The Happiness Factor

Jewish Wisdom for Happy Living

AUTHOR
Rabbi Mordechai Dinerman
in consultation with
David Pelcovitz, PhD

COURSE DEVELOPMENT
Rabbi Shlomie Chein
Mrs. Mushka Grossbaum
Rabbi Yanky Raskin
Rabbi Naftali Silberberg
Casey Skvorc, PhD

CURRICULUM COORDINATOR
Mrs. Rivki Mockin

ADMINISTRATOR
Rabbi Motti Klein
Mrs. Chana Zedek

LAYOUT AND DESIGN
Mrs. Vanessa Goldberg-Drossma
Mrs. Rivky Fieldsteel
Mr. Sam Griffin
Mrs. Shayna Grosh
Mrs. Chaya Mushka Kanner
Rabbi Motti Klein

THE ROHR JEWISH LEARNING INSTITUTE

CHAIRMAN
Rabbi Moshe Kotlarsky

PRINCIPAL BENEFACTOR
Mr. George Rohr

EXECUTIVE DIRECTOR
Rabbi Efraim Mintz

THE ROHR JEWISH LEARNING INSTITUTE

gratefully acknowledges the pioneering
and ongoing support of

George and Pamela Rohr

Since its inception, the Rohr JLI has been
a beneficiary of the vision, generosity,
care, and concern of the Rohr family.

In the merit of the tens of thousands of hours
of Torah study by JLI students worldwide,
may they be blessed with health, *Yiddishe
nachas* from all their loved ones, and
extraordinary success in all their endeavors.

Dedicated by

Dr. Gavriel and Pamela Ostrow

Chabad on Campus International and
the entire network of Chabad Houses
on campus around the globe salute the
Ostrows for their unwavering commitment
to benefiting the Jewish people.

May the Ostrow family go from strength to
strength and enjoy good health, overwhelming
happiness, and abundant prosperity!

Table of Contents

Endorsements

For a long time, when policy makers and educators asked me to develop programs or curricula to increase well-being in various field settings, I told them that there was not enough rigorous research to support such an endeavor. The day has come, however, that we are ready to apply the findings of positive psychology to the wider world! JewishU's *The Happiness Factor* is a thoughtful, impressive effort to accomplish just that. I wish I could take this course myself!

Sonja Lyubomirsky, PhD

Professor of Psychology at the University of California, Riverside
Author of *The How of Happiness* and *The Myths of Happiness*

JewishU's *The Happiness Factor* brings together modern research in positive psychology and ancient Jewish wisdom. This marriage between theology and science can bring about significant positive change in individuals and communities.

Tal Ben-Shahar, PhD

Lecturer, Interdisciplinary Center, Herzliya, Israel
Author of *Happier* and *The Question of Happiness*

The Happiness Factor provides a wonderful blueprint to help those who feel trapped in the past and to help release them to be in the moment. It is no secret. The pull of living in the past leads us into depression, while the preoccupation with the future keeps us anxious. Real calm and joy can only come from the present and being in the moment. I love this course and its step-by-step guide to achieve new feelings of positivity and optimism. It is practical and achievable.

Mark L. Brenner, PhD

Adjunct Professor, Pepperdine University
Founder of Parent Fitness Training

JewishU's *The Happiness Factor* presents an exciting integration of Jewish wisdom and several highly effective practices currently used in psychology. As a professional who has specialized in working with people whose life circumstances require unusual resiliency, I believe the combination of a Jewish spiritual approach along with positive psychology strategies promises to have far-reaching effects on individuals and their families. Both approaches are powerful alone in terms of enhancing well-being and together are likely to be synergistic in their impact.

Laura Marshak, PhD

Professor of Counseling,
Indiana University of Pennsylvania
Psychologist, North Hills Psychological Services
Author of *Married with Special-Needs Children*

I'm grateful to Professor Pelcovitz and JewishU for the gift of this essential and pioneering course on positive psychology. It will not only benefit us as individuals striving to lead a happy, creative, and joyful life; its teachings will also enhance our families, communities, and the world we live in, as we learn new strategies to deal with stressful times.

Harriet Lerner, PhD

Clinical Psychologist,
Lawrence, Kansas
Author of *The Dance of Anger* and *Marriage Rules*

The Happiness Factor helps us take this positive research and make it come alive. If more people were effectively educated on these topics, a revolution would occur as the world would know that happiness is a choice.

Shawn Achor

Author of *The Happiness Advantage* and *Before Happiness*

As a meaning scholar, I firmly believe that the best parts of our own humanity are drawn to a deep and true encounter with what really matters in life. JewishU's *The Happiness Factor* is a rich, accessible effort, embedding the science of positive psychology within the invaluable treasure of cultural and spiritual wisdom to facilitate the quest for meaning and fulfillment.

Michael F. Steger, PhD

Associate Professor, Colorado State University
Editor of *Purpose and Meaning in the Workplace* and *Designing Positive Psychology*

Positive psychology can only penetrate the individual in a lasting manner if it is consistent with their worldview. Therefore, aligning the scientific knowledge with cultural and spiritual roots is a wonderfully creative way to ensure long-term impact.

Ilona Boniwell, PhD

Principal Lecturer and Course Leader of MAPP (M.Sc. in Applied Positive Psychology), Anglia Ruskin University, Oxford, UK
CEO, Positran, Paris, France
Author of *Positive Psychology in a Nutshell*
Editor of *The Oxford Handbook of Happiness*

Positive psychology has shown the importance of activities and feelings such as thankfulness, forgiveness, and helpfulness in promoting positive mental health. Religion, spirituality, and virtue are starting to take their rightful place as scientifically and clinically sound sources of happiness. Building on exciting recent discoveries in positive psychology, participants in this course will discover strategies based on Jewish spiritual values for enhancing happiness. JewishU, Professor Pelcovitz, and all concerned can be congratulated for this initiative, which will make these important strategies accessible and usable for all taking part.

Kate Miriam Loewenthal, PhD

Emeritus Professor of Psychology,
Royal Holloway, University of London
Professor of Abnormal Psychology, NYU London

Once again, JewishU has hit the psychological bulls-eye. At a time when our vulnerability is increasing and our unease growing in the wrong direction, this course tackles the challenges to our well-being in a thoughtful, sensitive, and effective manner. A truly wonderful and helpful endeavor.

Rabbi Reuven P. Bulka, PhD, CM

Adjunct Professor, The College of the Humanities—Carleton University
Rabbi, Congregation Machzikei Hadas
Ottawa, ON, Canada

A proper education should include more courses like this one, which takes up basic questions of morality that are important to live a successful, mindful life.

Ellen Langer, PhD

Professor of Psychology, Harvard University
Author of *Mindfulness* and *Counterclockwise*

Course Foreward

By David Pelcovitz, PhD

I am honored to write the foreword for JewishU's course *The Happiness Factor,* an inspiring course that provides a synthesis of current findings from the field of positive psychology integrated with ancient Jewish wisdom. This melding of modern research with insights informed by Jewish learning can provide invaluable understanding and direction toward living an ethical, happy, and fulfilling life.

The relatively new discipline of positive psychology has signaled a paradigm shift in the mental health field. Instead of focusing on what is wrong with an individual, positive psychology systematically studies how to actively nurture strengths. At a practical level, this leads to empirical investigations into how to understand and promote happiness rather than alleviate depression. Positive psychologists are less interested in anger, while more concerned about forgiveness; they are more likely to try to understand gratitude rather than cynicism. One of the founders of positive psychology, Dr. Martin Seligman, points out that when parents dream of how they want their child to be as an adult, their focus is not on raising a child who is not depressed or anxious but on a child who embraces life with joy and enthusiasm.

This focus is very familiar to students of *Chasidut, Musar* (ethical teachings), and *Hashkafah* (Jewish thought). Traditionally, Jewish practice and learning have placed a great deal of emphasis on living a life filled with joy, gratitude, and virtually every other area that is the focus of positive psychology. Jewish texts are replete with wisdom that foreshadows many of the empirical findings of research and explores what it means to nourish positive emotion. A more nuanced understanding of the wisdom that Jewish thinkers have expressed about these virtues over the millennia would serve to enrich the field of positive psychology. Likewise, the emerging science of techniques on how to nourish these traits in educational, family, personal, and business settings may enhance Jewish thinking and living.

Surveys of American parents over the past thirty years consistently find that they view preparing children to become responsible citizens as one of the most important goals of education. An array of studies conducted over the last decade find that values emphasized by positive psychology are at least as important in predicting long-term success in children as are grades. For example, self-discipline is twice as good a predictor of high school grades as IQ. Furthermore, happy adolescents earn substantially more money as adults than their less happy counterparts. Researchers have also found that the skills and values imparted by an approach informed by positive psychology have been found to differentiate flourishing corporate teams, relative to stagnating teams, in the business world as well as predict greater satisfaction and success in one's personal relationships. For example, in the realm of marriage, an extensive series of studies conducted by John Mordecai Gottman and his colleagues have documented that a five-to-one ratio of positive to negative interactions is necessary for marriages to thrive.

I teach a required course on Jewish perspectives in positive psychology at the Azrieli Graduate School of Jewish Education at Yeshiva University. The reaction of my students to this course has consistently been excitement at how applying the lessons of positive psychology in Jewish settings shows much promise as an effective approach to leading a more fulfilling life. The designers of *The Happiness Factor* have brought together this approach in a highly effective and accessible manner. They have skillfully summarized the recent advances in positive psychology, while at the same time presenting the wisdom of Chasidic thought and Torah insights. All of this is done in a practical manner that can help bring higher levels of fulfillment and values-driven living into our daily lives.

David Pelcovitz, PhD

Gwendolyn & Joseph Straus Chair in Psychology and Jewish Education,
Azrieli Graduate School of Jewish Education and Administration, Yeshiva University

THE JOY OF HAVING

Finding Happiness
in Life's Gifts

We're often told that money can't buy happiness;
joy must come from within. But let's be honest:
are we really supposed to think that having nicer
things doesn't mean anything? And yet, we all
know that person who seems to have it all—and
is somehow still miserable. So which is it? Classic
Jewish sources suggest that what matters most
is how we appreciate our life circumstances and
how regularly we express that appreciation.

Exercise 1.1

One can be happier if . . .

Exercise 1.2

Subjective Happiness Scale

For each of the following statements and/or questions, circle the point on the scale that you feel is most appropriate in describing you.

I. In general, I consider myself:

| I | 2 | 3 | 4 | 5 | 6 | 7 |

not a very happy person   a very happy person

2. Compared with most of my peers, I consider myself:

| I | 2 | 3 | 4 | 5 | 6 | 7 |

less happy   more happy

3. Some people are generally very happy. They enjoy life regardless of what is going on, getting the most out of everything. To what extent does this characterization describe you?

| I | 2 | 3 | 4 | 5 | 6 | 7 |

not at all   a great deal

4. Some people are generally not very happy. Although they are not depressed, they never seem as happy as they might be. To what extent does this characterization describe you?

| I | 2 | 3 | 4 | 5 | 6 | 7 |

not at all   a great deal

Thousands of people have taken this questionnaire, and scientists have compared their scores. Here's how to arrive at your score.

First, reverse the score of the last question (but not the other three) as follows: A score of 7 becomes I, a score of 6 becomes 2, etc. Then add the four numbers and divide them by four.

Older adults average a score of 5.6. The college-age score is a bit below 5. Of course, to determine that your score is not transient, you need to do this exercise more than once, over the course of a few months.

Sonja Lyubomirsky, The How of Happiness (New York: Penguin Press, 2008), p. 33

TEXT 1

TAL BEN-SHAHAR, *HAPPIER: LEARN THE SECRETS TO DAILY JOY AND LASTING FULFILLMENT* (LONDON: MCGRAW-HILL, 2008), PP. IX–X

In the United States, rates of depression are ten times higher today than they were in the 1960s, and the average age for the onset of depression is fourteen and a half compared to twenty-nine and a half in 1960. A study conducted in American colleges tells us that nearly 45 percent of students were "so depressed that they had difficulty functioning." Other countries are following in the footsteps of the United States. In 1957, 52 percent in Britain said that they were very happy, compared to 36 percent in 2005—despite the fact that the British have tripled their wealth over the last half century. With the rapid growth in the Chinese economy comes a rapid growth in the number of adults and children who experience anxiety and depression. According to the Chinese Health Ministry, "The mental health status of our country's children and youths is indeed worrying."

While levels of material prosperity are on the rise, so are levels of depression. Even though our generation—in most Western countries as well as in an increasing number of places in the East—is wealthier than previous generations, we are not happier for it. A leading scholar in the field of positive psychology, Mihaly Csikszentmihalyi, asks a simple question with a complex answer: "If we are so rich, why aren't we happy?"

TAL BEN-SHAHAR, PHD

Noted teacher of positive psychology. Ben-Shahar currently teaches at the Interdisciplinary Center, Herzliya, Israel. He taught the largest course at Harvard University on positive psychology, and he consults and lectures around the world on the topics of leadership, education, ethics, happiness, self-esteem, resilience, goal setting, and mindfulness. He is the author of the international best sellers *Happier* and *Being Happy*, which have been translated into 25 languages.

TEXT 2

TIKUNEI ZOHAR 22

וְאַתְוָון בְּשִׂמְחָ"ה אִיהִי מַחְשָׁבָ"ה.

The letters forming the Hebrew word *besimchah* (with joy) are the same letters that spell *machshavah* (thought).

TIKUNEI ZOHAR

An appendix to the *Zohar*, the seminal work of kabbalah (Jewish mysticism). *Tikunei Zohar* consists mostly of seventy kabbalistic expositions on the opening verse of the Torah. It was first printed in Mantua in 1558.

TEXT 3

CHANIE GORKIN, "WORST DAY EVER?" WWW.POETRYNATION.COM

Today was the absolute worst day ever

And don't try to convince me that

There's something good in every day

Because, when you take a closer look,

This world is a pretty evil place.

Even if

Some goodness does shine through once in a while

Satisfaction and happiness don't last.

And it's not true that

It's all in the mind and heart

Because

True happiness can be attained

Only if one's surroundings are good.

It's not true that good exists

I'm sure you can agree that

The reality

Creates

My attitude

It's all beyond my control

And you'll never in a million years hear me say that

Today was a very good day.

Now read it from bottom to top, the other way,
And see what I really feel about my day.

CHANIE GORKIN
1998–

In 2015, when Chanie Gorkin
was in eleventh grade at Beth
Rivkah High School in Crown
Heights (Brooklyn, NY), she wrote
a poem for a school assignment.
The poem subsequently
went viral on social media.

Why does happiness have so many positive side effects?

TEXT 4

RABBI SHNE'UR ZALMAN OF LIADI, *TANYA*, CH. 26

בְּרַם כְּגוֹן דָּא צָרִיךְ לְאוֹדוּעֵי כְּלַל גָּדוֹל.

כִּי כְּמוֹ שֶׁנִּצָּחוֹן לְנַצֵּחַ דָּבָר גַּשְׁמִי, כְּגוֹן שְׁנֵי אֲנָשִׁים הַמִּתְאַבְּקִים זֶה עִם זֶה לְהַפִּיל זֶה אֶת זֶה, הִנֵּה אִם הָאֶחָד הוּא בְּעַצְלוּת וּכְבֵדוּת, יְנוּצַח בְּקַל וְיִפּוֹל, גַּם אִם הוּא גִּבּוֹר יוֹתֵר מֵחֲבֵרוֹ.

כָּכָה מַמָּשׁ בְּנִצָּחוֹן הַיֵּצֶר, אִי אֶפְשָׁר לְנַצְּחוֹ בְּעַצְלוּת וּכְבֵדוּת הַנִּמְשָׁכוֹת מֵעַצְבוּת וּטְמְטוּם הַלֵּב כָּאֶבֶן, כִּי אִם בִּזְרִיזוּת הַנִּמְשֶׁכֶת מִשִּׂמְחָה וּפְתִיחַת הַלֵּב וְטָהֳרָתוֹ מִכָּל נִדְנוּד דְּאָגָה וְעֶצֶב בָּעוֹלָם.

This should be made known as a cardinal principle:

The internal spiritual battle waged against one's negative impulses is similar to a physical wrestling match. If two individuals are wrestling with each other, each striving to fell the other, but one is lazy and lethargic, he will fall and be easily defeated, even if he is stronger than his opponent.

The same applies regarding the conquest of one's impulses. It is impossible to defeat them from a state of laziness and heaviness, which stem from sadness and a dull heart. They can be defeated only from a state of enthusiasm, which derives from happiness and a heart free of any trace of worry and sadness.

TEXT 5

RABBI SHALOM DOVBER SCHNEERSOHN, *SEFER HAMAAMARIM* 5657, PP. 221–222

טֶבַע הַשִּׂמְחָה הוּא לִפְרוֹץ גֶּדֶר. דְּהַיְינוּ כָּל הַגְדָּרָה וְהַגְבָּלָה שֶׁבַּנֶּפֶשׁ, טֶבַע הַשִּׂמְחָה הִיא לִפְרוֹץ הַהַגְדָּרָה וְהַהַגְבָּלָה הַהִיא ...

דְּכָל כֹּחַ כְּשֶׁבָּא לִידֵי גִּילוּי וְהַמְשָׁכָה . . . הֲרֵי הוּא בָּא בְּאֵיזֶה צִיּוּר, שֶׁנִּתְגַּלָּה
בְּאוֹפֶן כָּזֶה וְכָזֶה, וְהַצִּיּוּר הוּא הַהַגְבָּלָה . . . וְהַשִּׂמְחָה פּוֹרֶץ גֶּדֶר הַהַנְהָגָה
הָרְגִילָה, מִפְּנֵי שֶׁמוֹצִיאָה עֶצֶם הַכֹּחַ מִן הַהֶעְלֵם אֶל הַגִּילּוּי, וְעַל יְדֵי זֶה
הוּא יוֹצֵא מֵהַנְהָגָתוֹ הַגְּדוּרָה.

RABBI SHALOM DOVBER SCHNEERSOHN
(RASHAB) 1860–1920

Chasidic rebbe. Rabbi Shalom
Dovber became the 5th leader
of the Chabad movement
upon the passing of his father,
Rabbi Shmuel Schneersohn.
He established the Lubavitch
network of *yeshivot* called Tomchei
Temimim. He authored many
volumes of Chasidic discourses
and is renowned for his lucid
and thorough explanations
of kabbalistic concepts.

The nature of joy is to breach barriers. That is, joy tends to break through the various limitations and restrictions of the human character....

When the faculties of a person first emerge from a state of potential,... they each take a certain definition and shape.... Human joy breaks through this default state. When we are joyous, we tap into and reveal the deeper but latent potential of our character, and we are then empowered to behave in a different, enhanced manner.

TEXT 6

ZOHAR 2:184B

תָּא חֲזֵי: עָלְמָא תַּתָּאָה קַיְּימָא לְקַבְּלָא תָּדִיר . . .

וְעָלְמָא עִלָּאָה לָא יָהִיב לֵיהּ אֶלָּא כְּגַוְונָא דְּאִיהוּ קַיְּימָא. אִי אִיהוּ קַיְּימָא
בִּנְהִירוּ דְּאַנְפִּין מִתַּתָּא, כְּדֵין הָכִי נַהֲרִין לֵיהּ מֵעֵילָּא, וְאִי אִיהוּ קַיְּימָא
בַּעֲצִיבוּ, יָהֲבִין לֵיהּ דִּינָא בְּקִבְלֵיהּ.

כְּגַוְונָא דָא (תְּהִלִּים ק, ב) "עִבְדוּ אֶת ה' בְּשִׂמְחָה", חֶדְוָה דְּבַר נָשׁ מָשִׁיךְ
לְגַבֵּיהּ חֶדְוָה אַחֲרָא עִלָּאָה.

ZOHAR

The seminal work of kabbalah,
Jewish mysticism. The *Zohar* is a
mystical commentary on the Torah,
written in Aramaic and Hebrew.
According to the Arizal, the *Zohar*
contains the teachings of Rabbi
Shimon bar Yocha'i, who lived in
the Land of Israel during the 2nd
century. The *Zohar* has become
one of the indispensable texts
of traditional Judaism, alongside
and nearly equal in stature to
the Mishnah and Talmud.

Come and observe! Our world is always ready to receive [the spiritual flow that emanates from above]....

The upper world provides in accordance with the state below. If the state below is joyous, abundance flows from above; but if the state below is one of sadness, the flow of blessing is constricted.

Therefore, "Serve G-d with joy" (Psalms 100:2).

TEXT 7

RABBI MOSHE LEIB OF SASOV, *LIKUTEI RAMAL*, VAYETSEI

הַשִּׂמְחָה . . . מַדְרֵגָה יוֹתֵר מִבְּכִיָּה.

כִּי לְהַבְּכִיָּה פָּתוּחַ הַשַּׁעַר, כְּמוֹ שֶׁאָמְרוּ חֲכָמֵינוּ זִכְרוֹנָם לִבְרָכָה (בָּבָא מְצִיעָא נט, א) "שַׁעֲרֵי דְמָעוֹת לֹא נִנְעֲלוּ". אַךְ הַשִּׂמְחָה מְשַׁבֵּר הַמְּחִיצָה וְהַגּוּדָא.

Joy . . . is loftier than tears.

The heavenly gates remain open for our tears, as the Talmud says (Bava Metsi'a 59a), "The gates of tears are not locked." Joy, however, demolishes and pulverizes the [supernal] walls and barriers.

RABBI MOSHE LEIB OF SASOV
1745–1807

Chasidic rebbe. Rabbi Moshe Leib was a prominent disciple of Rabbi Shmelke of Nikolsburg and later went on to be one of the greatest disseminators of Chasidism throughout Eastern Europe. He was famous for his love and care for the downtrodden and was known as "the father of widows and orphans." One of his descendants published his teachings, a commentary on the Talmud and the Torah, in the 20th century.

TEXT 8

RABBI BACHYA IBN PAKUDAH, *CHOVOT HALEVAVOT*, INTRODUCTION TO *SHAAR HABECHINAH*

וּמְשָׁלָם בָּזֶה לְתִינוֹק, שֶׁמְּצָאוֹ אִישׁ אֶחָד מֵאַנְשֵׁי הַחֶסֶד בַּמִּדְבָּר, וְחָמַל עָלָיו, וַיַּאַסְפֵהוּ אֶל בֵּיתוֹ, וַיְגַדְּלֵהוּ, וַיַּאֲכִילֵהוּ, וַיַּלְבִּשֵׁהוּ, וַיִּתְנַדֵּב עָלָיו בְּכָל הַטּוֹב לוֹ, עַד שֶׁהִשְׂכִּיל וְהֵבִין אוֹפַנֵּי דַרְכֵי טוֹבָתוֹ.

וְאַחַר כֵּן שָׁמַע הָאִישׁ הַהוּא עַל אָסִיר שֶׁנָּפַל בְּיַד שׂוֹנְאוֹ, וְהִגִּיעָהוּ אֶל תַּכְלִית הַצַּעַר, וְהָרָעָב, וְהָעֵרוֹם יָמִים רַבִּים, וְנִכְמְרוּ רַחֲמָיו עַל צַעֲרוֹ, וּפִיֵּיס לְשׂוֹנְאוֹ, עַד שֶׁהִתִּירוֹ וּמָחַל לוֹ אֶת דָּמָיו, וַיַּאַסְפֵהוּ הָאִישׁ אֶל בֵּיתוֹ, וְהֵיטִיב לוֹ בְּמִקְצָת הַטּוֹב אֲשֶׁר הֵיטִיב בּוֹ לַתִּינוֹק.

A parable:

There was once an infant found in the desert by a kindhearted individual. This benevolent person took pity on the child, carried him home, brought him up, fed him, clothed him, and provided him generously with all that was good, until the child was old enough to understand and comprehend the many benefits he had received.

RABBI BACHYA IBN PAKUDAH
11TH CENTURY

Moral philosopher and author. Ibn Pakudah lived in Muslim Spain, but little else is known about his life. *Chovot Halevavot (Duties of the Heart)*, his major work, was intended to be a guide for attaining spiritual perfection. Originally written in Judeo-Arabic and published in 1080, it was later translated into Hebrew and published in 1161 by Judah ibn Tibbon, a scion of the famous family of translators. Ibn Pakudah had a strong influence on Jewish pietistic literature.

The same benefactor heard of someone who had fallen into the hands of his enemy and had for a long time been treated with extreme cruelty, starved, and kept naked. The benevolent person appeased the enemy and convinced him to free the prisoner and forgive his debt. The kind individual brought the man to his home, but the kindness provided to this man was a fraction of the kindness shown to the infant.

QUESTION FOR DISCUSSION

Which of the rescued individuals will be more appreciative of the rescuer? Why?

TEXT 9

HELEN KELLER, "THREE DAYS TO SEE,"
***ATLANTIC MONTHLY*, JANUARY 1933**

Only the deaf appreciate hearing, only the blind realize the manifold blessings that lie in sight. Particularly does this observation apply to those who have lost sight and hearing in adult life. But those who have never suffered impairment of sight or hearing seldom make the fullest use of these blessed faculties. Their eyes and ears take in all sights and sounds hazily, without concentration and with little appreciation. It is the same old story of not being grateful for what we have until we lose it, of not being conscious of health until we are ill.

I have often thought it would be a blessing if each human being were stricken blind and deaf for a few days at some time during his early adult life. Darkness would make him more appreciative of sight; silence would teach him the joys of sound....

Recently I was visited by a very good friend who had just returned from a long walk in the woods, and I asked her what she had observed. "Nothing in particular," she replied. I might have been incredulous had I not been accustomed to such responses, for long ago I became convinced that the seeing see little.

HELEN ADAMS KELLER
1880–1968

American author, political activist, and lecturer. Keller was the first deaf-blind person to earn a bachelor of arts degree. The story of how Keller's teacher, Anne Sullivan, taught her how to communicate has become widely known through the dramatic depictions of the play and film, *The Miracle Worker*. A prolific author, Keller was well-traveled and outspoken in her convictions. She campaigned for women's suffrage, labor rights, and socialism.

TEXT 10

MIDRASH, *KOHELET RABAH* 1:13

אֵין אָדָם יוֹצֵא מִן הָעוֹלָם וַחֲצִי תַּאֲוָתוֹ בְּיָדוֹ.

אֶלָּא אִן אִית לֵיהּ מֵאָה, בָּעֵי לְמֶעֱבַד יַתְהוֹן תַּרְתֵּין מָאוָון. וְאִן אִית לֵיהּ תַּרְתֵּי מָאוָון, בָּעֵי לְמֶעֱבַד יַתְהוֹן אַרְבָּעָה מְאָה.

We don't manage to leave this world with even half of our desires fulfilled.

When we have one hundred, we want to turn it into two hundred; when we have two hundred, we want to make of it four hundred.

QUESTIONS FOR DISCUSSION

- ► What is the cause for this human trait?

- ► What are the benefits of this trait?

- ► What are its drawbacks?

KOHELET RABAH

A Midrashic text on the Book of Ecclesiastes. Midrash is the designation of a particular genre of rabbinic literature. The term "Midrash" is derived from the root *d-r-sh*, which means "to search," "to examine," and "to investigate." This particular Midrash provides textual exegeses and develops and illustrates moral principles. It was first published in Pesaro, Italy, in 1519, together with 4 other Midrashic works on the other 4 biblical *Megilot*.

TEXT 11

RABBI SHALOM DOVBER SCHNEERSOHN, *SEFER HAMAAMARIM* 5659, P. 5

כְּשֶׁמְדַבֵּר דִּבְרֵי אַהֲבָה, שֶׁהַדִּיבּוּר מְקַבֵּל אָז מִמִּדַת אַהֲבָה שֶׁבְּנַפְשׁוֹ, הִנֵּה אָנוּ רוֹאִין שֶׁהַדִּיבּוּר מוֹסִיף אוֹר בְּהָאַהֲבָה, שֶׁעַל יְדֵי שֶׁמְדַבֵּר בָּהּ מֵאִיר בּוֹ הָאוֹר הָאַהֲבָה בְּיוֹתֵר וּמִתְפָּעֵל בְּיוֹתֵר בְּנַפְשׁוֹ בְּאַהֲבָה וְחִיבָּה לְהַדָּבָר הַהוּא . . .

וְכֵן הוּא בְּכָל הַמִּדוֹת: כְּשֶׁאֵינָם בָּאִים בְּדִבּוּר, יִתְקַטֵּן וְיִתְמַעֵט הִתְפַּעֲלוּת הַמִּדוֹת עַד שֶׁמִּתְעַלְמִים לְגַמְרֵי. וּלְהֵיפֵךְ עַל יְדֵי שֶׁבָּאִים בְּדִבּוּר, מִתְרַבִּים וּמִתְרַחֲבִים בְּיוֹתֵר.

When a person pours feelings of love into words, the act of speaking these words fuels and intensifies the love. Through speaking about it, the emotional energy radiates with more passion, and the person is aroused with more love and fondness for the beloved....

The same applies to all emotions: When they are not expressed through speech, they are reduced until they completely dissipate. When they are expressed verbally, they augment and grow considerably.

TEXT 12A

DEUTERONOMY 26:8–10

וַיּוֹצִאֵנוּ ה' מִמִּצְרַיִם בְּיָד חֲזָקָה וּבִזְרֹעַ נְטוּיָה וּבְמֹרָא גָּדֹל וּבְאֹתוֹת וּבְמֹפְתִים.

וַיְבִאֵנוּ אֶל הַמָּקוֹם הַזֶּה וַיִּתֶּן לָנוּ אֶת הָאָרֶץ הַזֹּאת אֶרֶץ זָבַת חָלָב וּדְבָשׁ.

וְעַתָּה הִנֵּה הֵבֵאתִי אֶת רֵאשִׁית פְּרִי הָאֲדָמָה אֲשֶׁר נָתַתָּה לִי ה'.

G-d brought us out from Egypt with a strong hand and with an outstretched arm, with great awe, and with miraculous signs and wonders.

He brought us to this place, and He gave us this land, a land flowing with milk and honey.

Now, behold, I have brought the first of the fruit of the ground that You, G-d, have given to me.

TEXT 12B

IBID., VERSE 11

וְשָׂמַחְתָּ בְכָל הַטּוֹב אֲשֶׁר נָתַן לְךָ ה' אֱלֹקֶיךָ וּלְבֵיתֶךָ.

And you shall rejoice in all the good that G-d has given you and your family.

TEXT 13

MIDRASH, *TANCHUMA*, KI TAVO 1

צָפָה מֹשֶׁה בְּרוּחַ הַקּוֹדֶשׁ וְרָאָה שֶׁבֵּית הַמִּקְדָשׁ עָתִיד לֵיחָרֵב וְהַבִּכּוּרִים עֲתִידִין לִיפָּסֵק, עָמַד וְהִתְקִין לְיִשְׂרָאֵל שֶׁיִּהְיוּ מִתְפַּלְלִין שְׁלֹשָׁה פְּעָמִים בְּכָל יוֹם.

Moses foresaw that the Temple would be destroyed and the offering of the first fruits would cease. He therefore ordained that the Jewish people should pray three times a day.

TEXT 14

SIDDUR, PRAYER UPON RISING IN THE MORNING

מוֹדֶה אֲנִי לְפָנֶיךָ מֶלֶךְ חַי וְקַיָּם, שֶׁהֶחֱזַרְתָּ בִּי נִשְׁמָתִי בְּחֶמְלָה. רַבָּה אֱמוּנָתֶךָ.

I thank You, living and eternal King, for mercifully restoring my soul within me. Your faithfulness is great.

TEXT 15

ROBERT A. EMMONS, *GRATITUDE WORKS!*
(NEW YORK: WILEY, 2013), PP. 23–24

In 1998 my colleague Mike McCullough and I designed a program of research to examine the effect of a gratitude practice on psychological and physical well-being. In our first study, we randomly assigned college student participants one of three tasks.... They either briefly described, in a single sentence, five things they were grateful for (the gratitude condition), five hassles (the hassles condition), or five events or circumstances that affected them (events condition). Hassles are relatively minor, everyday stressful circumstances such as not being able to find a babysitter, dealing with the rising price of gas, doing laundry, misplacing one's wallet. The time frame for each of these was the past week. Participants completed these exercises along with a variety of other measures of health and happiness once per week for ten consecutive weeks....

The results were quite striking.... Participants in the gratitude condition felt better about their life as a whole and were more optimistic about the future than participants in either of the other control conditions. To put it into numbers, they were a full 25 percent happier than the other participants. Those in the gratitude condition reported fewer health complaints and even spent more time exercising.... Something as simple as counting blessings once a week resulted in significant emotional and health benefits.

ROBERT EMMONS, PHD
1958–

Professor of psychology. Emmons teaches at the University of California, Davis, and is a leading scientific expert on the psychology of gratitude. Emmons is the founding editor in chief of *The Journal of Positive Psychology* and the author of multiple volumes on the subject of gratitude, including *Thanks! How Practicing Gratitude Can Make You Happier.*

Exercise 1.3

1. On a scale of 1–10, how proficient am I at being grateful for the things I have?

1	2	3	4	5	6	7	8	9	10

virtually not at all   enormously

2. What do I find most challenging about being grateful and expressing gratitude?

3. What piece of advice can I give myself to overcome this challenge?

4. In what way can I grow in terms of feeling and expressing more gratitude?

Key Points

1 The letters forming the Hebrew word *besimchah* (with joy) are the same letters that spell *machshavah* (thought). Happiness is a product of our thought processes and attitudes—not our circumstances.

2 In fact, happiness leads to success in many areas of life. This is because:

   a. It is easier to accomplish difficult tasks from a state of enthusiasm and happiness.

   b. While we are blessed with many talents and strengths, their full power often remains dormant. Joy drives our potential to flow outward.

   c. When we are happy, we create joy in the divine realm. This supernal ecstasy results in the flow of increased blessings.

3 Abundance and success do not necessarily lead to more happiness, because:

   a. When we have been surrounded by a superabundance of blessings since our youth, we tend not to notice them.

   b. Furthermore, when we obtain something new, we experience a spike of joy. But as we quickly adapt to the fresh circumstance, the joy withers away. This is why humans have an unquenchable thirst for more—we crave a repeat of that temporary spike of joy.

4 When emotions are not verbally expressed, they are diminished and they dissipate. When they are verbally expressed, they flourish and are amplified. By focusing on and talking about the blessings in our lives, we foster happy emotions; by focusing less on what we are missing, we allow our negative feelings to dissipate.

5 Ritualizing gratitude at fixed intervals allows us to reap happiness from that which we have. Judaism has a built-in system of rituals that facilitates a steady expression of gratitude for all of the blessings in our lives.

6 We ought to be grateful not only for the gifts we have, but also for the fact that they are provided by Someone Who cares. Realizing that G-d loves us and cares for us is, perhaps, an even greater source of happiness than the gifts themselves.

Appendix

TEXT 16

SUNIYA S. LUTHAR, "THE CULTURE OF AFFLUENCE: PSYCHOLOGICAL COSTS OF MATERIAL WEALTH," *CHILD DEVELOPMENT* **74:6 (2003)**

One of the first empirical studies to provide a glimpse into problems of affluent youth was a comparative investigation of low-income, urban 10th graders and their upper socioeconomic status (SES), suburban counterparts.... The sample included 264 suburban students who were mostly from Caucasian, white-collar families, and 224 inner-city youth who were predominantly minority and of low SES.... Affluent youth reported significantly higher levels of anxiety across several domains, and greater depression. They also reported significantly higher substance use than inner-city students, consistently indicating more frequent use of cigarettes, alcohol, marijuana, and other illicit drugs.

SUNIYA SUNANDA LUTHAR, PHD

Professor of psychology. Luthar is currently at Arizona State University and is professor emerita at Columbia University's Teachers College. Her books include *Children in Poverty, Developmental Psychopathology,* and *Resilience and Vulnerability in Childhood.* She served as associate editor of the journal *Developmental Psychology* and currently serves as associate editor for the journal *Development and Psychopathology.*

TEXT 17

SONJA LYUBOMIRSKY, *THE HOW OF HAPPINESS* **(NEW YORK: PENGUIN PRESS, 2008), P. 140**

As we acquire income and consumer goods that we desire, (e.g., gadgets, computers, cars, homes, or swimming pools), our aspirations simply rise to the same degree, thereby trapping us in a hedonic treadmill.

In one study that surveyed people over a thirty-six-year period, respondents were asked how much income was needed by a family of four to "get along." The higher the person's income, the more they estimated was required for a family of four. Remarkably, the estimate for "get along" income increased almost exactly to the same degree as did actual income, suggesting that the more you have, the more you think you "need."

SONJA LYUBOMIRSKY, PHD

Leading expert in positive psychology. Dr. Lyubomirsky is professor of psychology at the University of California, Riverside. Originally from Russia, she received her PhD in social/personality psychology from Stanford University. Her research on the possibility of permanently increasing happiness has been honored with various grants, including a million-dollar grant from the National Institute of Mental Health. She has authored *The How of Happiness* and, more recently, *The Myths of Happiness.*

I. A LIGHTNING ROD TO THE SPIRITUAL REALMS

RABBI SHLOMA MAJESKI

The positive potential of *simchah* is highlighted by the Maggid of Mezeritch's interpretation[1] of the teaching in *Pirkei Avos*:[2] "Know what is above you." Literally, the *Mishnah* is teaching us always to be conscious that, allegorically speaking, in the spiritual realms there exists an eye that sees everything we do, an ear that hears everything we say, and a hand that records everything that takes place.

The Maggid of Mezeritch extended the meaning of this teaching. He would say: "Know that everything above," all that transpires in the spiritual realm, is "from you," dependent on your conduct. Each of us influences what goes on in the spiritual realm. And so, when a person is happy, he not only lifts the spirits of the people around him, but he generates joy in the spiritual realm as well.

Let us explain the dynamics at work: One of the most fundamental concepts discussed in the *Kabbalah* and in *Chassidic* philosophy is the interrelationship between the spiritual realm and our material reality. The *Zohar*[3] states that our material world parallels the spiritual realm. It is like a mirror reflecting an object or person before it. When one sees a person moving a hand in the mirror, one realizes that standing in front of the mirror is an actual person who is moving his hand. Even when we cannot see the person himself, the image in the mirror is sufficient.

Similar concepts apply with regard to the interrelation between the physical and spiritual realms. Our physical realm mirrors spiritual reality. Everything taking place on our plane has a parallel within and gives us an understanding of the workings of spiritual existence. Although we may not be directly conscious of spiritual reality, we can understand many things about it from the parallels we see in our world.

This concept also has a deeper dimension. When we are speaking of a mirror and a person, we are talking about two separate, unrelated entities; one merely reflects the other. With regard to the spiritual and the physical, it is not that the spiritual realm is one form of existence and the physical realm another, with G-d creating them to correspond to each other. In this instance, the two are more closely related. Our material existence is merely an extension of the spiritual.

We do not have a proper analogy to illustrate this. One of the closest examples we have is the relationship between the soul and the body. Our Sages tell us[4] that just as the soul fills up the body, G-d fills up the world. Therefore, if we want to develop a better understanding of the interaction between G-d and the world or in different words, the spiritual realm and the physical realm we can focus on the relationship between the body and the soul, the *neshamah* and the *guf*.

The activity of a person's soul is reflected in his body. If a person is anxious, you can tell by looking at him. One look at his eyes and his facial expression tells the whole story. The same is true when he is angry and when he is sad. And surely this is true when he is happy. When a person is truly *b'simchah*, his face radiates joy. For what a person experiences internally expresses itself in his physical form.

It has to be this way. The soul and the body function as a single entity. Although they have different sources, as long as a person is alive, his body and his soul share a single identity, and the body expresses what is happening within the person's soul.

A similar concept applies with regard to the interaction between the spiritual realm and the physical realm. When we see something happening in the physical realm—for example, it is raining—what we are seeing is, in essence, a reflection of what is taking place in the spiritual realm. In the spiritual realm, there is a great outpouring of kindness, and that becomes manifest in our world as rain.

And this holds true for all the events that take place in our world, a snowfall, a wind, an earthquake. From the most unusual to the most mundane, everything that occurs in our world is a result and a reflection of something that is taking place in the spiritual realm.

RABBI SHLOMA MAJESKI

Scholar of Chasidic philosophy. Rabbi Majeski serves as the dean of Machon Chana Women's Institute in Crown Heights, Brooklyn, and is the author of *The Chassidic Approach to Joy* and *A Tzaddik and His Students*.

There is, however, a dual nature to the dynamic of causation. Just as what happens in our material realm is a result of what is taking place in the spiritual realm, what takes place in the spiritual realm can be determined by the events of our world. This is the meaning of the teaching of the Maggid of Mezeritch mentioned above. He explained that the *Mishnah* in *Pirkei Avos* is telling us to: "Know that what is above," the goings on in the spiritual realm, "is from you," dependent on our conduct. We mortals determine the nature of the influences active in the spiritual realm.

Why does man have this potential? Because "man was created in the image of G-d."[5] Needless to say, this does not mean that G-d has the same physical form as man; G-d is infinite and He has no body or shape whatsoever.[6] *Chassidus* and *Kabbalah*, nevertheless, explain that there is a spiritual counterpart to all our bodily features. G-d does not possess eyes, but He possesses a means of perception that operates in a more complete way than we could possibly comprehend in a manner comparable to our power of sight. He does not possess a mouth, but He possesses a means of expression that corresponds to our power of speech. Similarly, every element of our being has its counterpart in the spiritual realm.

And so, when we move our hands, we are also activating the spiritual counterpart of our hands. Everything we do, all of our activities and everything that goes on in our lives in this physical realm, has an effect in the spiritual world.

In particular, there are three phases in this cycle: our deeds, the effect that activity has in the spiritual realm, and the reflection of the activity within the spiritual realm in our material world.

For example, when someone is not well, G-d forbid, and a friend decides to give charity in his merit, the friend's gift activates G-d's attribute of *chessed* (kindness) in the spiritual realm. This in turn becomes manifest in our world in the improvement of the sick person's condition.

The Baal Shem Tov explains a similar idea,[7] commenting on the verse,[8] "G-d is your shadow." Literally, the verse tells us that just as a shadow protects us from the sun, G-d shields us. The Baal Shem Tov, however, offers an extended interpretation, explaining that just as a shadow mirrors a person's actions, the nature of the influence that flows from G-d to the world will be a reflection of the nature of our activities.

This same idea is reflected in the Maggid's interpretation of the *Mishnah*, "Know what is above you," that "what is above" is dependent on "you." Everything that happens in the spiritual realm is determined by our behavior, because whatever we do activates the counterpart in the spiritual realm. And that spiritual activity brings about changes in our world. When I show compassion to another person that motivates G-d to show compassion.

Let us take another example of this idea. When two people marry, their union reflects the creation of a similar bond in the spiritual realm. For within the spiritual realm, there are two aspects: one referred to as *Malchus*, which reflects the feminine dimension, and another, referred to as *Zaer Anpin*, which reflects the masculine dimension. When a man and woman marry, they bring about a union between these attributes in the spiritual realm. This union, in turn, encourages the flow of positive influence to our material world.

Similar concepts apply with regard to speech. Everything said in our realm activates a counterpart in the spiritual realm. So when we say good things, positive influences are generated in the spiritual realm. And if, G-d forbid, we say unfavorable things, negative influences are generated.

This is one of the explanations of our Sages' statement,[9] "Do not regard the blessing of an ordinary person lightheartedly." We know that blessings given by a *tzaddik*, a righteous person, can bring about miraculous changes in our lives. But the truth is that whenever anyone gives a blessing, the blessing has power. For the person's statements create effects not only in our world, but in the spiritual realm. When he speaks words of blessing, he is actually generating a blessing in the spiritual realm. And that blessing can effect change in our world.

(The converse is also true. And for this reason, the Torah forbids cursing another person. For this can also, Heaven forbid, have an effect.)

Our thoughts also effect changes in the spiritual realm. In this world, thought has no apparent effect, but the dynamic of spiritual causation is such that every expression of our being, be it thought, speech, or action, creates a spiritual effect. And that spiritual effect can later bring about changes in our world. Indeed, we find that intense thought about another person has often produced very positive effects.[10]

There was once a *chassid* whose son was very ill. After a prolonged illness, the physicians finally told him that there was no hope. There was nothing more they could do; they did not know if the child would live.

The *chassid* was devastated. He hurried to Lubavitch and approached the Tzemach Tzedek, the third Lubavitcher Rebbe. Overcome with grief, he could barely mouth his request for a blessing.

The Rebbe answered him briefly in Yiddish: *Tracht gut, vet zein gut*. "Think positively, and the outcome will be good."[11]

As the *chassid* walked out of the Rebbe's room, he pulled himself together. He put himself in a state of mind that radiated utter confidence. He knew G-d could help him and cure his son. And he believed that this would happen.

When he came home, he was told that there had been a sudden change in his son's condition. The physicians had no explanation, but the child had definitely taken a turn for the better. When the *chassid* inquired, he was told that the change took place at exactly the time that he visited the Rebbe.

The story shows us that thinking positively produces two effects:

  a) when a person is in high spirits, he functions better; and

  b) thinking positively itself brings about positive change. By envisioning good in one's mind, one creates positive spiritual influence that enables that picture to materialize.

This is the basis of the *Chassidic* explanation of one of the most fundamental principles of Judaism, *bitochon*. *Bitochon* means confidence and trust that G-d will help. That G-d can help us at any given time is a point of faith, and one that is very easy to accept. After all, if He is G-d, He is capable of doing anything He wants. *Bitochon* means more than that; it expresses our trust and confidence that He will actually help.

Bitochon is not euphoric escapism; it does not absolve an individual of taking responsibility for his future, and acting accordingly. It means that as a person acts, he realizes that his efforts are dependent on G-d's providence, and he relies on G-d and trusts Him totally.

Besides giving a person the confidence and inner strength to face challenges, this approach also generates positive Divine influence. When a person trusts and relies on G-d, G-d creates situations that will allow him to use his energies in positive and beneficial ways.[12] Our positive thoughts serve as catalysts that promote favorable circumstances for us.

Now we can appreciate the importance of *simchah*. When a person is genuinely happy and sees things in a positive way, he creates *simchah* in the spiritual realm, for "everything that happens above is dependent on you."

The joy that is activated in the spiritual realm is not self-contained, but flows outward, bringing joy to many others in our world. When we are *b'simchah*, in both a physical and spiritual way, we bring joy to ourselves, our families, and all the people around us.

As we explained in the previous chapter, this joy is not a passive potential. On the contrary, "joy breaks through barriers," destroying all the obstacles and difficulties that may present themselves.

When a person is happy, he stands above all his personal limitations and weaknesses. He can do things that he ordinarily could not do. He can forgive his worst enemy. His joy generates inner energy that breaks through and shatters any barrier that stands in his way.

When a person creates joy in the spiritual realm, the same thing happens. In the spiritual realm, there are also limitations and barriers, for G-d has chosen to establish a natural order through which He controls our world. Just as there are rules of nature that govern the physical world around us, there are principles of causality that govern the effects produced by our conduct. For as above, everything we do generates an effect in the spiritual realm that in turn produces an effect within our world. On the most general level, these rules follow the following principle:[13] When a person does good, he receives benefits that enable him to continue in this path. If he fails to do good, he will suffer difficulties that make it obvious to him that he should change his ways. These are the patterns of causation that G-d chose to establish in the spiritual realm.

Nevertheless, when a person is *b'simchah*, he creates joy in the spiritual realm; G-d Himself is, so to speak, also *b'simchah*. This causes G-d to reveal a transcendent dimension that is not bound by the laws of causation mentioned above. In simple terms, this means that G-d will give great blessings and make positive things happen, even though normally these blessings would not be granted.

When, G-d forbid, there is a situation where something is not going right, we must realize that this is a result of the laws of causation that G-d established. We must, however, also realize that by radiating *simchah*, we can awaken *simchah* above, and effect a radical change in the situation before us.

This demonstrates the power our joy possesses. With *simchah* we can change the makeup of the spiritual realm, and in this manner, bring blessing and all forms of good to ourselves, our families, and to the entire Jewish people.

The Chassidic Approach to Joy (New York: Sichos in English, 1996), pp. 97–105

Reprinted with permission of the publisher

Endnotes

1. Cited in *Or HaTorah al Aggados Chazal*, p. 112b.

2. 2:1; See *In the Paths of Our Fathers*, p. 43 (Kehot, N.Y., 1994).

3. I, 38a, 205b; c.f. *Berachos* 58a; *Zohar* I, 197a, III, 176b.

4. *Berachos* 10a.

5. *Genesis* 1:27.

6. See *Rambam, Mishneh Torah, Hilchos Yesodei HaTorah* 1:7–12.

7. *Keser Shem Tov, Hosafos* 60.

8. *Tehillim* 121:5.

9. *Berachos* 7a.

10. *Likkutei Dibburim*, Vol. I, p. 6 (English translation).

11. See *Sefer HaSichos 5687*, p. 113 and sources cited there; explained in *Likkutei Sichos, Parshas Shemos 5751*.

12. See *Sefer HaIkkarim*, Discourse 4, Chapter 47.

13. See *Rambam, Hilchos Teshuvah* 9:1.

2. CELEBRATING LIFE

RABBI JONATHAN SACKS

Not Taking Life for Granted

It happened on our honeymoon. We had decided to go to Switzerland. I had always wanted to see the mountains, to climb high and breathe the chill air. It was beautiful in theory, and it was no less lovely when we arrived. The valley was bathed in light. The mountains looked down on us in majesty.

The next day we got ourselves ready for a climb and went outside. The mountains had disappeared, the one thing we had not reckoned on had happened. It was raining. The mountains had retreated behind a covering of low cloud. Gamely, for a few days, we climbed, wrapped in mist and dampness through which nothing could be seen. Eventually we decided it was too miserable. 'Let's try somewhere else', we said. So we hitchhiked down to Italy where we found the sun.

We stayed in a little coastal town called Paestum, an ancient place with some fine Roman ruins. And the sea. Rarely had it seemed more inviting than just then, after the gloom of Switzerland. The trouble was . . . I could not swim. It was not that I had never tried, but somehow I just could not get the hang of it.

As we sat on the beach and looked out across the water, however, I realized that the shore must be sloping very gently indeed. People were far out into the sea and yet the water was only coming up to their knees. It looked safe just to walk out, and so it was. I walked out to where I had seen people standing just a few minutes before and the water gently lapped against my knees. Then I started walking back to the shore. That was when it happened. Within minutes I found myself out of my depth.

How it happened I am not sure. There must have been a dip in the sand. I had missed it on my way out, but walked straight into it on my way back. I tried to swim. I failed. I kept going under. I looked around for some possible source of rescue. The

other people bathing were a long way away—too far to reach me, I thought, too far to even hear. Besides which, we were in Italy. As I went under for the fifth time, I remember thinking two thoughts: 'What a way to begin a honeymoon!' and 'What's the Italian for "help"?'

It is difficult to recapture the panic I felt. Clearly someone rescued me, or I would not be writing now. At the time, however, it did seem like the end. As far as I can reconstruct that moment in my memory, I had already reconciled myself to drowning when someone, seeing me thrashing about, swam over, took hold of me and brought me to the shore. He deposited me, almost unconscious, at the feet of my wife. I was too shocked to do or say anything. I never found out his name. Somewhere there is someone to whom I owe my life.

It changed my life. For years afterwards, I would wake in the morning conscious of the fact that but for a miracle, I would not be here. Somehow that made everything easier to bear. Our life has had difficult times. It has had moments of crisis. Public life is full of stress and not everyone who lives it has a thick skin. People often ask me, 'How do you bear it?' The answer is simple. That day, on an Italian beach, I learned that life, which I so nearly lost, had been given back to me. It is difficult to feel depressed when you remember fairly constantly that life is a gift.

This is why, every morning, I say with real feeling the traditional Jewish prayer on waking up: 'I thank you, living and everlasting King, for restoring my soul to me in compassion, great is your faithfulness.' Thank you G-d, for giving me back my life.

It was then that I realized something I should have understood long before. Faith is not a complex set of theological propositions. It is simpler and deeper than that. It is about not taking things for granted. It is a sustained discipline of meditation on the miracle of being. 'Not how the world is, but that it is, is the mystical,' said Wittgenstein. Not how we are, but *that* we are, is cause for wonder, and faith is the symphony on that theme.

We are here. We might not have been. Somehow that makes every day a celebration, for at the core of that mystical awareness is the discovery that life itself is the breath of G-d. . . .

RABBI JONATHAN SACKS, PHD (1948–2020)

Former chief rabbi of the United Kingdom. Rabbi Sacks attended Cambridge University and received his doctorate from King's College, London. A prolific and influential author, his books include *Will We Have Jewish Grandchildren?* and *The Dignity of Difference*. He received the Jerusalem Prize in 1995 for his contributions to enhancing Jewish life in the Diaspora, was knighted and made a life peer in 2005, and became Baron Sacks of Aldridge in 2009.

Giving Thanks

Oliver James's book *Britain on the Couch* tells a depressing story. Quite simply, we have become more depressed. Twenty-five-year-olds today are between three and ten times more likely than their parents to have suffered some form of depressive illness. We have become, in James's phrase, a 'low serotonin society'—serotonin being the chemical register in the brain of general states of well-being.

Depressive illness is tragic and needs serious medical attention. James's book though, raises a larger question. Can there be, he asks, something in our culture that has given rise to this sudden increase? Admittedly, it will not explain individual cases, only trends, but the question is real and has a long history. Just as there can be a physically unhealthy society, so there can be a psychologically unhealthy one.

James argues that part of the blame lies with the chaos of intimate relationships, especially in the breakdown of the stable two-parent family. No less important, though, are the kinds of emotions favoured by a commercial, competitive society. 'Advanced capitalism,' he says bluntly, 'makes money out of misery and dissatisfaction.'

Paraded daily before us on our television screens and in our newspapers are images of perfection, people who are more beautiful, thin, clever, or attractive that we will ever be. Ours is a culture of artificially created longings. We are invited to resolve the tension by buying this, or wearing that, or going there. Unhappiness is good for business. It just happens to be bad for people.

At this stage, the religious believer wants to protest that it need not be like this at all. It is not a matter of opposing capitalism and all its works. It has, after all, made possible much of what makes life more dignified for more people than ever before. Economic growth and technological progress have allowed us to treat disease, conquer absolute poverty and extend the possibilities of travel and communication. Never before has so much been available to so many. The best cure for nostalgia is to imagine going to the dentist in any previous historical era. There is nothing wrong in celebrating the achievements of advanced societies.

There is, however, one spiritual discipline which religion once gave us and which we still need. It is the simple act of saying 'thank you' to G-d. There are prayers in which we ask G-d for the things we do not have, but there are others in which we simply thank G-d for the things we do have: family, friends, life itself with its counterpoint of pleasure and pain, the sheer exaltation of knowing that we are here when we might not have been.

To thank G-d is to know that I do not have less because my neighbor has more. I am not less worthwhile because someone else is more successful. Through prayer I know that I am valued for what I am. I learn to cherish what I have, rather than be diminished by what I do not have. A third-century rabbi put it simply. 'Who is rich?' he asked. Not one who has much, but 'one who rejoices in what he has'.

There is no single route to happiness, just as there is no single cure for depression, but the daily discipline of thanking G-d for what we are and what we enjoy is the most ancient form of what is today called 'cognitive therapy'. Making a blessing over life is the best way of turning life into a blessing.

Celebrating Life: Finding Happiness in Unexpected Places (London: Continuum International Publishing Group, 2003), pp. 7–9, 14–16

3. GRATITUDE

RABBI RAPHAEL PELCOVITZ, DAVID PELCOVITZ, PHD

What is the origin of the name "Jew," *Yehudi*? Why are we not called "Hebrew," *Ivri*, or "Israelite," *Yisraeli*, as we were classified in earlier times? The reason, according to our teachers, is because the root of the name Yehudah is *hodaah*, to thank, to express gratitude. Judah was the fourth son of Leah and she felt a profound sense of gratitude when he was born. There was a tradition that Jacob was destined to have twelve sons, who would comprise the twelve tribes of Israel. Since Jacob had four wives, it was assumed that each wife would be allocated three sons.

When Leah gives birth to a fourth son, she is overwhelmed with a sense of thanksgiving:

> *She conceived again, and bore a son and declared, "This time let me gratefully praise Hashem"; therefore she called his name Judah; then she stopped giving birth.*[1]

Rashi comments:

> *"I have taken more than my share, so I now need to give thanks."*

A Jew must always feel this same sense of gratitude to G-d, continually recognizing that he is the recipient of heavenly blessings. This attribute is the antithesis of a sense of entitlement. A Jew must acknowledge that he is a debtor who owes so much to his past— to his forebears and his progenitors; he is not a creditor to whom something is owed. This attribute of gratitude is reflected in his name, his identity, and shapes his essential character: *Yehudi*.

RABBI RAPHAEL PELCOVITZ (1921–2018)

Rabbi emeritus, author, and teacher. Rabbi Pelcovitz served as the pulpit rabbi and community leader of Congregation Kneseth Israel (the White Shul) in Far Rockaway, New York, for more than 50 years. He authored a number of books in which he presents ideas from Jewish thought in a compelling and comprehensible way. He also co-authored 2 books with his son, Dr. David Pelcovitz.

DAVID PELCOVITZ, PHD

Psychologist, teacher, and author. Dr. Pelcovitz, who received his PhD from the University of Pennsylvania, has published and lectured extensively on a variety of topics related to education, parenting, and mental health. He is currently the Straus Professor of Psychology and Education at the Azrieli Graduate School, Yeshiva University. His books include *Balanced Parenting* and *Life in the Balance*, both written in collaboration with his father, Rabbi Raphael Pelcovitz.

Another indication of the enormous importance that Jewish thought places on our obligation to express gratitude is the following *midrash*:

> *In the future, all offerings will be abolished except for the thanksgiving-offering. All prayers will be abolished except for prayers of gratitude.*[2]

Given the central role that offerings and prayer serve in Jewish life, this *midrash* is teaching us the central significance of gratitude. The need to express gratitude will remain even at a time that other spiritual duties and obligations will no longer be necessary.

Our Rabbis teach us that a key aspect of the experience of bringing the *korban todah* (thanksgiving-offering) is the social component. When one brought a thanksgiving-offering— which was offered after being saved from a life-threatening situation—he was required to bring 40 loaves of bread, 10 each of four different forms. One of each kind was given to the Kohen, leaving 36 loaves to be consumed within a time frame including that day and the ensuing night. The medieval classic commentator on the Torah, the Sforno,[3] explains that this was to ensure that at the time that one expressed gratitude for his good fortune, one had no choice but to make this a social event. Included in this occasion was sharing one's food while recounting to others the story of the life-saving incident.

In *Alei Shur*,[4] Rabbi Wolbe further develops this interpersonal component of gratitude. He discusses the importance of overtly expressing feelings of gratitude to others as a means of fanning the flames of love and friendship between one Jew and another. He cites the Talmud[5] which states that if one gives bread as a gift to a child, it is important to inform the child's parents who gave the gift. As Rashi explains, identifying the source of this kindness evokes feelings of love and gratitude between Jews.

The need to express one's gratitude is also noted by secular thinkers. British novelist and academic C.S. Lewis said:

> *I think we delight to praise what we enjoy because the praise not merely expresses but completes the enjoyment; it is its appointed consummation.*[6]

Gratitude has an individual, more personal, component. In addition to the need to overtly express feelings of appreciation to those who have been kind to us, we also have to internally nourish an emotional awareness of gratitude toward G-d. The only segment of the *Amidah* (or *Shemoneh Esrei*, the 19-blessing prayer recited three times a day) that can't be delegated to the *chazzan* during his repetition of the *Shemoneh Esrei* is *Modim*: the part of this prayer that focuses most directly on expression of gratitude to G-d for all that He has done for us as individuals and as a people. This is because when it comes to giving thanks to G-d, we can't delegate to others. Each individual has to articulate his own declaration of gratitude in a manner that fosters an internal recognition of gratitude.

Rabbi Wolbe also discusses this facet of gratitude, which is more related to individual as opposed to interpersonal growth. He elaborates on the *midrash*[7] that explains that Aharon, not Moshe, invoked the plagues that involved water and land. The reason for this was because it wasn't proper for Moshe to show any signs of ingratitude to the water that saved his life as an infant, or to the earth that allowed him to hide the Egyptian he killed when defending his fellow Jews. Obviously inanimate objects have no feelings that need protection. The reason why Moshe had to delegate these plagues to his brother was to develop in himself feelings of gratitude toward the vehicles of his salvation.

This aspect of gratitude was seen in a very concrete and moving way by those who visited Rabbi Yisroel Zev Gustman at Yeshivah Netzech Yisroel in Jerusalem. Rabbi Gustman always insisted on carefully caring for the trees and bushes in his garden, even though his students frequently offered to help him perform these seemingly menial gardening chores. He explained that during the war, he hid from the Nazis in a forest where the shelter of the bushes and the fruit of the trees repeatedly saved his life. He felt that caring for these trees and bushes was a necessary expression of gratitude to these instruments of his survival.

Further insight into the primary importance of the expression of gratitude is provided by the following analysis of Rabbi Joseph Soloveitchik regarding the connection between gratitude, prayer, and man's sustenance from nature.[8] In the Torah's discussion of the Creation, the following passages describe the creation of vegetation and precipitation:

Now all the plants of the field were not yet on the earth, and all the herbs of the field had not yet sprouted; for Hashem G-d had not sent rain upon the earth, and there was no man to work the soil.[9]

Rashi, on this verse, points out that rain didn't come to earth until man was there to pray for it. In essence, Rashi says, the "switch" for rain is activated by prayer and gratitude, not the other way around:

Why didn't it rain? Because man wasn't there to work the land, and there was no one to recognize the benefit of rain. When man came and recognized that rain was a necessity for the world, he prayed for it and rain came down, allowing trees and grass to grow.

Rashi interprets the lack of rain and vegetation to the lack of recognition on anyone's part to acknowledge the goodness and beneficence of G-d. When Adam was created, he recognized and acknowledged the great blessing and benefit of rain. Subsequently, when Adam prays for rain, his prayers serve as a trigger for rain to fall and that results in the growth of vegetation. All this is alluded to in the word *siach ha'sadeh*—the plant of the field. The word "*siach*," translated as vegetation of the field, refers not only to vegetation but also to prayer. We find this term in reference to Isaac's prayers, where the term *lasuach* is used.[10] The meaning of these verses, according to Rabbi Soloveitchik, is that since there was no concept of prayer in the world until the creation of man, there was no spark to ignite the force of rain. This phenomenon can only occur when man acknowledges and expresses his gratitude for this gift.

Psychological Perspective

Secular thinkers also describe the central role that gratitude has in living a moral life. Cicero, the ancient Roman philosopher, described gratitude as a cornerstone of all values, writing that: *"Gratitude is not only the greatest of virtues, but the parent of all the others."*[11]

At first glance, being thankful does not logically seem to be of such central importance relative to the many other virtues for which people strive. Nevertheless, recent psychology research on the impact of building gratitude into one's life clearly confirms the importance of cultivating this trait.

Studies have found numerous benefits that stem from building the capacity for gratitude into daily living. Those who regularly express gratitude are more likely to be forgiving, generous, agreeable and less likely to be narcissistic and selfish.[12] Research repeatedly confirms that those with high scores on measures of gratitude also score high on measures of happiness. In one study, 95 percent of individuals describe feeling happy when expressing gratitude and over 50 percent say that expressing gratitude made them feel *extremely happy.*[13]

From the viewpoint of parents and educators, a number of benefits result from teaching our children to be thankful. As a purely practical matter, when children express gratitude it makes it more likely that their benefactor will continue to act kindly toward them in the future. Perhaps more importantly, from the perspective of character education, the expression of gratitude also makes it more likely that the recipient will be generous to others.[14] Interestingly, this research finding suggests that a pathway to teaching our children to be giving and charitable is inculcating in them the value of *hakaras ha'tov,* gratitude. Perhaps by focusing their attention on thankfulness for what they receive, we develop their ability to give.

Ingratitude

A story was told to me (RP) by a congregant, regarding his father who was a prominent member of a Brooklyn synagogue many years ago:

> *His father was an extremely kind and generous man who did favors for countless people. He noticed that a fellow congregant, whom he considered a friend, was acting strangely toward him, conveying a general attitude of resentment. Troubled by this behavior he said to him: "Reb Yankel, why are you angry at me? I haven't done you a favor yet!"*

This congregant told me that he learned a great lesson from this episode: When doing a kindness for another, there is often a duality of emotions created between the recipient of a favor and the benefactor.

Researchers have found that most individuals find feelings of indebtedness to be unpleasant. Many individuals are uncomfortable with feeling dependent on others. A favor creates an inherent sense of discomfort; it forces one to reciprocate and feel obliged. The recipient is now a debtor, he owes his benefactor and that makes him uncomfortable, so he tries to minimize and belittle the favor. Rabbi Shimshon Dovid Pincus points out that the Hebrew expression for ingratitude—*kafui tov*—is related to the Hebrew word *kafah,* meaning to be forced or pressured. For example, the Rabbis tell us that if an individual resists fulfilling an obligation in a religious court, the court is authorized to pressure him until he acquiesces. The term for this is *kofim oso*—they pressure or force him. Similarly, when the Jews were given the Torah at Sinai and were reluctant, at first, to accept, the *Midrash* says *kafah aleihem*—G-d suspended the mountain over them, threatening to annihilate them unless they agreed. Based on this, Rabbi Pincus submits[15] that, frequently, when a favor is done for a person, he feels obligated and even pressured to pay back the debt of gratitude that he owes to his benefactor. This creates a sense of imbalance, an uncomfortable feeling of dependence fueled by a sense of indebtedness and a need to reciprocate. This character trait is traced by the Sages to the beginning of time and to Adam at Creation.

Instead of expressing gratitude when given the gift of Chavah, the first woman, Adam blames her when confronted by G-d after defying His command to not eat the fruit of the Tree of Knowledge. Adam's first line of defense when accused of eating this fruit is to blame her by saying:

The woman whom You gave to be with me gave me of the fruit of the tree etc. . . .[16] The Talmud[17] comments on this episode by pointing out the irony of how swiftly gratitude can turn to ingratitude.

Rabbi Yechezkel Sarna[18] describes how a tendency toward ingratitude is built in as a default setting in the basic nature of man. He cites a *midrash* that explains why the word *adam* is used in the passage describing the punishment meted out to the generation that built the Tower of Bavel: *Hashem descended to look at the city and tower which the bnei Adam built.*[19] This *midrash* explains that the inherent nature of man includes, as mentioned above, this tendency toward a lack of gratitude. Instead of expressing eternal gratitude for having been saved from the deluge, this subsequent generation rebels against G-d. They build a tower, which our Sages explain was motivated by a desire to storm the heavens and prevent G-d from sending future destructive forces upon mankind. Apparently the innate sense of gratitude that one should feel toward his benefactor is tinged with an underlying sense of thanklessness. Therefore, one has to be very careful to not allow this innate tendency toward being a *kafui tov* to overtake him.

The following anecdote illustrates this tendency:

A grandmother is watching her grandchild play on the beach when a huge wave comes and washes him out to sea. She lifts her eyes to heaven and pleads, "Please, G-d, save my only grandson, bring him back!" A big wave washes the boy back onto the beach, good as new. The grandmother looks up to heaven and accusingly says: "He had a hat."

Our sense of gratitude is often incomplete. There is a tinge of the "ingrate" in us, because we somehow feel that what has been granted to us is incomplete.

Rabbi Yitzchak Hutner, reflecting the writings of the *Maharal* on the seriousness of ingratitude, writes of the seriousness of failing to be grateful:

When a person receives a benefit from his fellow, a seed of chesed is planted in his world. If the nature of chesed is functioning healthily and properly, this seed cannot but give rise to additional chesed. But if the person is an ingrate, it is as if he uproots the sprouting of chesed with his bare hands. Without a doubt, uprooting a planting of chesed is even more antithetical to the essence of chesed than is simply being uninvolved in matters of chesed. . . . An ingrate damages and destroys the very attribute of chesed. . . . One who is ungrateful to his fellow, it is as if he is ungrateful to G-d, because his denial is a response not just to the particular act of chesed that was done for him, but also to the attribute of chesed in the broadest sense.[20]

In light of this interpretation of ingratitude, it is not surprising to find the following statement made by the *Maharal:*

It is forbidden to do acts of chesed for one who will not respond with gratitude. For this reason, it didn't rain until man was created to pray for the rain.[21]

To the extent that ingratitude is viewed as heresy, the *Maharal's* position is understandable. One is not allowed to put an individual in a position where he is, in essence, ungrateful to G-d and simultaneously undermining one of the basic building blocks of humanity.

Habituation

The enemy of gratitude is habituation. The way the human brain works is that we quickly become accustomed to even the most spectacular of gifts.

I (DP) gave a paper at a beautiful resort in Hawaii. Surrounded by magnificent waterfalls, spectacular scenery, and unforgettable sunsets, I engaged one of the hotel staff in conversation. I asked him if it is possible to ever get used to working in such a remarkable setting. He answered: "To me this is just a job, I don't notice the beauty anymore. I drag my feet coming to work every Monday morning just like everybody else."

Related to this aspect of human nature is the unfortunate reality that we tend to be least grateful to those who are closest to us. Research on the psychology of gratitude has found that people tend to be more grateful for the unexpected. Human nature is such that we experience less gratitude for favors done for us by family and close friends than when somebody who we are less close to does the same favor.[22]

The tendency toward habituation is also seen in the relationship between man and G-d. In the classic work *Duties of the Heart* (*Chovos HaLevavos*), Rabbeinu Bachya details the reasons for our ingratitude to G-d:

People . . . grow up surrounded with a superabundance of Divine favors which they experience continuously, and to which they become so accustomed that they come to regard these as essential parts of their being, not to be removed or separated from themselves during the whole of their lives. When their intelligence develops and their mental faculties become strong, they foolishly ignore the benefits the Creator has bestowed on them and do not consider the obligation of gratitude for Divine beneficence, for they are unaware of the high degree of the boon. . . .[23]

Contrast this to the following incident that beautifully illustrates how, in the face of an extremely stressful chronic situation, individuals can show gratitude for even the most basic human experience:

At a retreat for families of children with severe cognitive and physical limitations, I (DP) met with a family who had an 8-year-old daughter who was born with such profound brain damage that she was unable to speak or engage in even the most basic self-care functions. Her mother told me that for the first four years of her daughter's life she was unable to sit up, and the family was given little hope that this most basic of human activities would ever be possible. The child's parents heard of a program overseas that offered intensive physical therapy for their daughter's condition, having some limited success in working with these children. After years of visits to this program their daughter was now able to sit up. The parents called over the counselor who was caring for their daughter at the retreat and with intense excitement showed me how this 8-year-old daughter was now able to see the world from the perspective added by her newfound ability to sit. The girl flashed a million-dollar smile at her parents who met the smile with tears of pride and gratitude.

The obvious lesson taught by these remarkable parents is that it is possible to have gratitude for even the most basic of gifts given to us on a daily basis. The challenge is finding a way, under normal circumstances, to continually remind ourselves, as Rabbeinu Bachya writes, of the "*superabundance of Divine favors which we experience continuously.*" Developing awareness of what to be grateful for even when life is going smoothly can require conscious effort and constant practice. As noted by Rabbi Sarna, without practice, this trait will not flow naturally from man's innate tendencies. The default setting is habituation.

Developing a Habit of Attention:
Finding Beauty and Meaning in the Mundane
The passage in the Torah regarding gifts to the poor while working in the fields is incongruously placed in the middle of the Torah's section discussing the various festivals and holidays in the Jewish calendar. After teaching us the laws regarding Pesach and Shavuos, followed by the laws of Rosh Hashanah, Yom Kippur, and Succos, there is a strange and incongruous interruption in the theme of the Torah's text by the insertion of the commandment regarding gifts to the poor:

> *When you reap the harvest of your land, you shall not remove completely the corners of your field as you reap and you shall not gather the gleanings of your harvest; for the poor and the*

proselyte shall you leave them; I am Hashem, your G-d.[24]

What is the significance of this interpolation? The *baalei Mussar* explain that when a Jew makes his pilgrimage to Jerusalem on one of the festivals, he is exposed to one of the highpoints of the Jewish experience. He senses the excitement and vibrancy of tens of thousands of Jews gathered from the four corners of Israel, joining in the observance of a Pesach and Shavuos. As a spectator, he stands in awe and reverence beholding the service of the Priests and the beautiful music and singing of the Levites. He is truly on a high and inspired beyond description. Reality, however, must soon set in when he leaves the holy city and goes back to his workshop or farm and is suddenly cast from the heights of spirituality to the physical, material life of the craftsman or farmer. He is challenged to retain spirituality in his mundane, day-to-day activities. That is why the Torah injects the laws of sharing one's produce with the less fortunate in the midst of the festival portion. It reminds the Jew that the moments of exhilaration and spiritual highs must be carried over and applied to the fields and mundane living. The commandments of G-d are common to both arenas. The material and the physical can be infused and informed by the spiritual experiences that he had when he went on his pilgrimage.

By the same token, what inspired the non-Jew to reject his way of life and his beliefs and decide to convert to Judaism? In Jewish theology we never encourage proselytizing; on the contrary, we try to dissuade a non-Jew from converting, explaining to him the rigorous disciplines he will be subjected to as a member of the Jewish faith. We are always very frank and open with him regarding the strictures of Jewish law. Still it seems strange that while we give him instructions in the fundamentals of Judaism if we are convinced of his sincerity to become a convert, the Talmud tells us that of all of the commandments of the Torah it is these obligations to the poor that we must teach a convert before the process of conversion is complete:

> *If a prospective proselyte comes to a Jewish court to convert to Judaism in the present era . . . we inform him of the sin of failing to observe the laws of* leket *(leaving gleanings for the poor),* shichchah *(leaving forgotten sheaves for the poor), and* pe'ah *(the part of the harvest left over in the corner of the fields).*[25]

Why is such importance given to this particular commandment? It is to teach the convert that while the inspiration that motivated him to convert is understandable—emanating either from a charismatic teacher or his experience witnessing special Jewish events, such as the majesty of the Jewish holidays or Jewish practice in the home on a Shabbos or festival—this enthusiasm and exuberance can easily ebb and wane when he must confront the reality of day-to-day living. It is for this reason that we teach him the laws that operate when he has come down from the mountain of spiritual heights to the field of the routine. We are teaching him that Jewish ideals are expressed in the tedious and the mundane, even as it is true of the special majestic moments of life. This may well be termed "the ordeal of the ordinary," which must in all frankness be taught to the prospective proselyte.

Developing a Habit of Attention

Breathing is the most natural and reflexive continuous action of a person. The Sages, noting the similarity between the Hebrew word *neshamah* (soul) and the Hebrew word *neshimah* (breath), comment on the verse, *Let all souls praise G-d,*[26] man should praise and thank the Almighty for every breath.[27] This is the ultimate example of their awareness of continually working on the need to overcome the tendency toward habituation.

Psychologists tell us that the antidote to habituation is consciously being mindful of how fortunate one's condition is and how it could have been otherwise.

While not easy, we can develop a habit of awareness, a habit of attention.

Gregg Krech, an author and counselor who specializes in the psychology of gratitude,[28] walks us through a disastrous Monday morning that is destined for catastrophe from the moment the alarm clock fails to wake us, all the way through to a near-death experience driving to work. The series of mishaps culminates when faced with an angry tirade from the boss after arriving so late for work. It is only when things go wrong that our attention is grabbed. It takes such an "out of the ordinary" event to bring us to an awareness and appreciation of a "normal" day. Krech points out: "What would happen if we turn the story around and experience a day when the alarm goes off as intended and you arrive at work without unexpected traffic or accidents?" How do we cultivate an approach to life that pays attention to the expected?

Perhaps the most potent antidote to habituation, from a Jewish perspective, is the daily experience of prayer. One-third of the prayers in the daily service address the theme of gratitude. What can be a more powerful answer to the challenge posed by Krech than thanking G-d three times a day with words expressing gratitude for the "miracles that surround us every day"? Of course, this too is a challenge. It is difficult to concentrate on the meaning of words said during prayer, and many experience the need to emotionally connect to the meaning of these words as a continual challenge. However, as we discussed, there are multiple spiritual and emotional benefits that emerge from concentrating on connecting to prayer in a manner that cultivates a habit of attention to that for which we should be grateful.

Rabbi Chaim Shmulevitz[29] discusses the dangers of *tardeimas ha'heirgeil*, the deep sleep brought on by habituation. Overcoming this requires that we cultivate a fresh look at what has become too familiar. He illustrates this with the following incident depicted in the Talmud:

> *Rav Alexandri went to the marketplace and called out: "Who wants life, who wants life?" All the people came and gathered round him saying: "Give us life!" He then quoted to them, "Who is the man who desires life and loves his days so that he may see good in them . . . Guard your tongue from evil and your lips from speaking deceit."*[30]

What was Rav Alexandri telling people that they didn't already know? Among the practical lessons that Rav Alexandri was teaching was that when widely known information to which we might have become habituated is presented in a novel way, we can view it with fresh eyes in a manner that develops the habit of attention to what has otherwise become ordinary.

Cynicism

An enemy of gratitude is cynicism. To the extent that gratitude requires a focus on the positive, cynicism is characterized by sarcasm, suspicion, and scorn.

There is an interesting question posed by the *Meshech Chochmah* regarding the passage in the Torah that describes the punishment of a man who cursed G-d:

And Moses spoke to the Children of Israel, and they took the blasphemer to the outside of the camp, and they stoned him to death; and the Children of Israel did as Hashem had commanded Moses.[31]

The *Meshech Chochmah* asks why it says "as commanded"; after all, the Jews did many things at Hashem's command. Why single out the incident of the blasphemer for saying this?

He answers that a cynical complainer can cool off one's enthusiasm. The blasphemer scoffed regarding the miracle of the Showbread. "Do you serve a king week-old bread?" he asked mockingly. There is always a danger when one is exposed to a complainer that a seed of doubt is planted regarding one's zeal and commitment to what one is doing. The passage therefore tells us that the complaints of the blasphemer did not impact the enthusiasm of the Jews in carrying out G-d's command in performing the mitzvah of the Showbread. It does not refer to the carrying out of the sentence, but to their retention of loyal obedience to G-d's commandment that had been challenged by the sinner.

Secular Perspectives on Cynicism

Research in the workplace has found that cynicism thrives when one feels disappointed in oneself or others, and becomes disillusioned because of being treated in a manner that breeds distrust, frustration, and resentment.[32] It is not surprising that when cynicism dominates in a family or one's job, motivation is sapped and antagonism increases.[33]

Reality television programs and sitcoms are often replete with cynical remarks, particularly when younger characters interact with their elders. What is particularly alarming is how common it is on sitcoms for children to be depicted as being chronically cynical, portraying this type of worldview as admirable and worthy of emulation. The findings of the Josephson Institute systematically document how this influence has impacted our children. In their 2009 survey of over 7,000 participants, the Josephson Institute of Ethics found alarming trends documenting the rise of cynicism in the United States. This institute has been taking the moral pulse of residents of the United States every two years since 1992. In their most recent survey, they report evidence that "The hole in the moral ozone seems to be getting bigger—each new generation is more likely to lie and cheat than the preceding one."[34] Adolescents, in 2009, were found to be five times more likely, and young adults three times more likely, than those over 40, to cynically endorse the belief that one must lie and cheat in order to be successful in life. This is a particularly ominous finding since their research confirmed that those who believe that cheating is necessary are significantly more likely to cheat or lie when they become adults. Those who cheat as adolescents were also found to be significantly more likely when adults to lie to their spouses, customers, employers, and insurance companies. It is of note that in this survey, participants who said that religion is an important part of their life tend to be less cynical than those who say that religion is not important (13 percent vs. 18 percent). The obvious take-home message is that this alarming trend can be checked to the extent that parents and educators shield children from excess exposure to media that glorify cynicism. Needless to say, parents, educators, and other adults in a child's life must always be aware of their vital function as role models and act accordingly. Following some of the suggested recommendations below regarding cultivating gratitude should also serve to lessen the tendency toward cynical attitudes and behavior.

Recommendations for Fostering Gratitude

1. *Counting One's Blessings*—An important study regarding the benefits of gratitude suggests an intervention that can help to effectively build awareness of what we should be grateful for in our daily lives.

In this study, over the course of ten weeks, participants were assigned to one of three groups:

a Subjects who were asked to write about five things they were grateful for during the past week.

b Participants were asked to enumerate five hassles from the past week.

c Subjects were asked to list five events that affected them.

In the ensuing period, research participants who were assigned to the gratitude group felt better about their lives as a whole, were more optimistic about the future, reported fewer health complaints, and exercised more.

The actual script used in this study is informative:[35]

At the beginning and end of each day, list five things for which you are grateful, and then take a few minutes to meditate on the gift inherent in each. One means of elucidating this sense of appreciation is the use of the following sentence stem: "I appreciate __ because __." In the first blank, list the person, event, or thing for which you are grateful, and in the second blank state the reasons for each of the things for which you have expressed gratitude. Discuss the effects of one week of this practice with a classmate, and tweak the exercise as you wish.

More recently, researchers have found that this technique is as beneficial for children and adolescents as it is for adults.[36] For example, in one study, adolescents were given the following instructions:

There are many things in our lives, both large and small, that we might be grateful about.
Think back over the past day and write down up to five things in your life that you are grateful or thankful for.

In that study, the adolescents experienced improved levels of optimism, life satisfaction, and overall satisfaction with school relative to adolescents in a comparison group. In a review of the research measuring the efficacy of this technique,[37] researchers summarize seven studies that found significant increases in feelings of well-being when one thinks about what they should be grateful for in this systematic manner. Of course, it isn't necessary to write down what one is grateful for on a list. Going around the table during Friday-night meals and asking family members to share what they are grateful for that week can reap similar benefits. This has the added advantage of increasing family members' knowledge of details about each other's life—a benefit that has independent advantages according to research in family psychology.[38]

2. ***Direct Expression of Gratitude***—Directly expressing thanks leads to even more dramatic benefits. In a study done by Seligman and his colleagues,[39] adults were given one week to write and then deliver a letter of gratitude in person to someone who had been especially kind to them but had never been properly thanked. Happiness levels of the individuals who carried out this exercise increased substantially for a month after they paid the visit to their benefactor.

A teacher was speaking to an 11th-grade student who said that her love of learning came from a third-grade teacher whose enthusiasm for teaching continued to inspire the student even eight years later. The teacher asked: "Did you ever thank your third-grade teacher or even let her know of the way she changed your life?" When the student answered, "No," the teacher immediately asked her to go into a private area of the school office to write a note expressing her gratitude to the teacher. Both the student and the recipient of the note described the experience as deeply meaningful.

3. Research has found that overcoming the natural tendencies that serve as impediments to gratitude can help cultivate a personality that is more likely to be grateful. The following characteristics serve as impediments to gratitude:

a) ***Self-preoccupation***—When one is so engrossed in their individual life-dramas, little room is left for one to notice the needs of others. This calls for developing the muscle of empathy and awareness of the needs and suffering of others, even when pulled into the inevitable hassles that accompany daily life.

In his biography of his teacher, Rav Yerucham Levovitz, Rabbi Wolbe relates a memorable story about the extent of his teacher's empathy. Rabbi Levovitz was told that a Jewish man was arrested by the Russians and accused of being a spy, an extremely serious offense that often resulted in the execution of the prisoner. It was reported that the level of Rabbi Levovitz's anguish was so great that when he awoke the morning after hearing the news, his beard had turned white.

b) ***Expectation***—Human nature is to expect whatever one has become accustomed to. We tend to no longer be grateful or attentive to something that is expected and routine. What gets our attention is when the expectation is not met. A possible antidote is to develop the habit of paying attention to the lessons learned when our expectations are not met. When one is confronted with periods of illness instead of expected good health, once one's health returns, it is doubly important to try to hold on to the feelings of gratitude for good health. Likewise, on a more mundane level, when luggage is lost by the airline and one has to live for several days without all the clothing one is accustomed to, he can redouble his efforts to more fully appreciate his wardrobe once the luggage is returned.

   c) *Entitlement*—The feelings of entitlement that often accompany the many luxuries of day-to-day life in an affluent society serve to block our awareness of how grateful we should be for the many gifts we regularly experience. When feelings of entitlement dominate, gratitude will, by definition, take a backseat. The antidote is to pay attention to the daily life of those less fortunate than we are. Periodic exposure to those living in poverty or with illness and disabilities, or those living in countries where basic civil liberties aren't respected, can serve as an important antidote to entitlement.

4. *Journal Keeping*—As noted earlier, systematically writing about what one is grateful for can have powerful benefits. There are many disciples of the early *baalei Mussar*, such as Rabbi Yisroel Salanter, Rabbi Yitzchak Blazer, and others, who have transmitted to their students either orally or in their writings that these great *Mussar* teachers had a practice of keeping what was called a *pinkus*—a notebook or diary—on their nightstand. They would record their experiences of the day and the lessons they learned from that day's activities, before retiring for the night.

In other cultures as well, such as Japan, there is a similar practice called "*Naikan.*" This is a way of life for many, marked by structured self-reflection that, in that culture, helps develop a sense of gratitude.

Practitioners of *Naikan* ask themselves the following three questions related to gratitude during their daily meditation:

1. What have I received from others?
2. What have I given to others?
3. What troubles and difficulties have I caused others?

Whether in writing or thought, a daily *cheshbon hanefesh* (self-assessment) that includes reflection on our levels of gratitude and transcendence of self-involvement can be an important aspect of developing this trait.

5. Although at first glance admitting to our mistakes is not linked to gratitude, on a deeper level cultivating such non-defensiveness can also help nourish a sense of gratitude. As Gregg Krech says: "As long as I am humbled by my own mistakes or limitations, I am more likely to receive what I am given with gratitude and a true sense of appreciation for the giver as well as the gift."[40]

6. Parents should remember the importance of modeling gratitude in order to teach their children. Since it is so difficult to maintain gratitude toward those to whom we are closest, continually reminding ourselves to express gratitude to one's spouse, family members, and close friends is an important component of educating our children in this important trait. As noted in our book, *Balanced Parenting*, instilling gratitude—by taking an extra moment to thank a salesclerk at the store, or tipping the paperboy for getting the paper on the porch every day—lets our children see that gratitude is part of the daily repertoire of social interaction.

Children should be reminded to thank parents for what they may take for granted; for example, help with homework, a lift to a friend's house, or taking them out to dinner. Parents should resist any tendency to inadvertently sabotage this lesson by responding with phrases like: "Don't mention it." Instead, the child should be praised for expressing gratitude. Acting as a role model by expressing gratitude to others, in front of your child, is another powerful lesson in instilling this core value.

Life in the Balance: Torah Perspectives on Positive Psychology (New York: Shaar Press, 2014), pp. 101–125

Reprinted with permission of the authors

Endnotes

1. *Genesis* 29:35.
2. *Vayikra Rabbah* 9.
3. *Leviticus* 7:12.
4. Rabbi Shlomo Wolbe, *Alei Shur*, Volume II, p. 279.
5. *Beitzah* 16a.
6. Lewis, C.S. (1996). *Readings for Meditation and Reflection.* New York: HarperOne.
7. *Shemos Rabbah* 9:9.
8. Rabbi Hershel Schachter (1994). *Nefesh HaRav—Torah from Rabbi Joseph B. Soloveitchik.* Hoboken, NJ: Ktav.
9. *Genesis* 2:5.
10. Ibid. 24:63.
11. Marcus Tullius Cicero, *Selected Works*, Penguin Classics (1960).

12. McCullough, M. & Emmons, R. (2004). *The Psychology of Gratitude*, Chapter 7, Oxford, UK: Oxford University Press.

13. Emmons R. & McCullough, M. (2003). Gratitude, optimism and health, counting blessings. *Journal of Personality and Social Psychology, 84*, p. 377.

14. Peterson & Stewart (1996). Antecedents and contexts of generativity. *Psychology and Aging, 11*, 21–33.

15. *Tiferes Shimshon Al HaTorah, Chukas.*

16. *Genesis* 3:12.

17. *Avodah Zarah* 5a.

18. Rabbi Yechezkel Sarna, *Delillas Yechezkel.*

19. *Bereishis Rabbah* 38:9 (on *Genesis* 11:5).

20. *Pachad Yitzchak, Rosh Hashanah,* # 3, translated by Dr. Shai Held.

21. *Gur Aryeh, Genesis* 2:5 *"v'ein makir b'tovosam."*

22. McCullough, M. & Emmons, R. (2004). *The Psychology of Gratitude*, Oxford, UK: Oxford University Press.

23. *Duties of the Heart (Chovos HaLevavos),* Introduction to Section Two, translation by Moses Hyamson (1999). New York: Feldheim.

24. *Leviticus* 23:22.

25. *Yevamos* 47a.

26. *Psalms* 150:6.

27. *Bereishis Rabbah* 14.

28. Krech, G. (2001). *Naikan: Gratitude and the Japanese Art of Self-Reflection.* St. Paul, MN: Stone Bridge Press.

29. *Sichos Mussar, Maamar* 97.

30. *Avodah Zarah* 19b, *Psalms* 34:13–14.

31. *Leviticus* 24:23.

32. Mirvis, P. & Kanter, D. L. (1991). Beyond demography: A psychographic profile of the workforce. *Human Resource Management, 30*(1), 45–68.

33. Mirvis, P. & Kanter, D. L. (1989). Combating cynicism in the workplace. *National Productivity Review, 8*(4), 377–394.

34. Character Study Reveals Predictors of Lying and Cheating, Press release. Josephson Institute of Ethics, October 29, 2009.

35. Script from *Emmons & McCullough* (2003).

36. Froh, J. J., Sefick, W. J. & Emmons, R. A. (2008). Counting blessings in early adolescents: An experimental study of gratitude and subjective wellbeing. *Journal of School Psychology, 46,* 213–233.

37. Wood, A., Froh, J. J. & Geraghty, A. (2010). Gratitude and well-being: A review and theoretical integration. *Clinical Psychology Review (30),* 890–905.

38. Gottman, J. (1999). *The Seven Principles for Making Marriage Work.* New York: Random House.

39. Seligman, M. E. P., Steen, T. A., Park, N. & Peterson, C. (2005). Positive psychology progress: Empirical validation of interventions. *American Psychologist, 60,* 410–421.

40. Krech, G. Exploring the link between gratitude and attention. To Do Institute (online).

THE JOY OF BEING YOU

Finding a Self-Concept of Happiness

Staying positive about life means staying positive about ourselves. In this second step, we look at the importance of nurturing a healthy self-concept and how to avoid negative feelings about ourselves. Oftentimes, it is feelings of nihilism and excessive navel-gazing that drags us down, but they can be countered by two prime, if paradoxical-seeming, Jewish principles: that I matter as an individual—but it isn't all about me.

Exercise 2.1
Rosenberg Self-Esteem Scale

Below is a list of statements dealing with your general feelings about yourself. Using the numbers 1–4 (1 = Strongly Disagree, 4 = Strongly Agree), indicate how strongly you agree or disagree with each statement.

	SCORE	REVERSE SCORE
I feel that I'm a person of worth, at least on an equal plane with others.		
I feel I have a number of good qualities.		
All in all, I am inclined to feel that I am a failure.		
I am able to do things as well as most other people.		
I feel I do not have much to be proud of, compared to most others		
I take a positive attitude toward myself.		
On the whole, I am satisfied with myself.		
I wish I could have more respect for myself.		
I certainly feel useless at times.		
At times I think I am no good at all.		

To determine your score, first "reverse score" the ratings of 3, 5, 8, 9, and 10. For these items only, change 1 to 4, 2 to 3, 3 to 2, and 4 to 1. Then add up the ten ratings and calculate the sum. The highest self-esteem score that you can get is 40; the lowest is 10.

Source: Morris Rosenberg, Society and the Adolescent Self-Image (Princeton, N.J.: Princeton University Press, 1965)

TEXT 1

DR. ABRAHAM J. TWERSKI, *LET US MAKE MAN: SELF ESTEEM THROUGH JEWISHNESS* (NEW YORK: CIS PUBLISHERS, 1991), PP. 8–11

Although many people are aware that they have little self-confidence and that they harbor feelings of inadequacy, they believe these feelings are justified because they are convinced their inadequacies are real. *Quite often, this self-perception is incorrect,* and the low self-esteem and poor self-confidence are in reality unjustified…. Many people see themselves as less than what they are in reality, and they are fully convinced that their perceptions are absolutely correct. Others' opinions to the contrary and even concrete evidence of their excellence may have little or no impact….

As I studied the negative self-image problem, I found that the most profound feelings of low self-esteem paradoxically occur most often in those who are in reality most gifted and competent. It appears that the person who develops a negative self-image sees himself as if he were looking through a trick lens which distorts the perception in such a manner that the person sees himself as the opposite of what he actually is.

RABBI ABRAHAM J. TWERSKI, M.D.
1930–

Psychiatrist and noted author. Rabbi Twerski is a scion of the Chernobil Chasidic dynasty and a well-known expert in the field of substance abuse. He has authored more than 50 books on self-help and Judaism and has served as a pioneer in heightening awareness of the dangers of addiction, spousal abuse, and low self-esteem. He served as medical director of the Gateway Rehabilitation Center in Pittsburgh and as associate professor of psychiatry at the University of Pittsburgh School of Medicine.

TEXT 2

NUMBERS 13:33

וְשָׁם רָאִינוּ אֶת הַנְּפִילִים בְּנֵי עֲנָק מִן הַנְּפִלִים, וַנְּהִי בְעֵינֵינוּ כַּחֲגָבִים וְכֵן הָיִינוּ בְּעֵינֵיהֶם.

There we saw giants of immense height. In our eyes, we seemed like grasshoppers, and we looked the same to them.

TEXT 3

GENESIS 1:27

וַיִּבְרָא אֱלֹקִים אֶת הָאָדָם בְּצַלְמוֹ, בְּצֶלֶם אֱלֹקִים בָּרָא אֹתוֹ, זָכָר וּנְקֵבָה,
בָּרָא אֹתָם.

G-d created humankind in His image, in the image of G-d He created him; male and female He created them.

TEXT 4

MISHNAH, SANHEDRIN 4:5

לְפִיכָךְ נִבְרָא אָדָם יְחִידִי, לְלַמֶּדְךָ שֶׁכָּל הַמְאַבֵּד נֶפֶשׁ אַחַת מִיִּשְׂרָאֵל מַעֲלֶה
עָלָיו הַכָּתוּב כְּאִלּוּ אִבֵּד עוֹלָם מָלֵא, וְכָל הַמְקַיֵּים נֶפֶשׁ אַחַת מִיִּשְׂרָאֵל
מַעֲלֶה עָלָיו הַכָּתוּב כְּאִלּוּ קִיֵּים עוֹלָם מָלֵא . . .

וּלְהַגִּיד גְּדֻלָּתוֹ שֶׁל הַקָּדוֹשׁ בָּרוּךְ הוּא, שֶׁאָדָם טוֹבֵעַ כַּמָּה מַטְבְּעוֹת
בְּחוֹתָם אֶחָד וְכֻלָּן דּוֹמִין זֶה לָזֶה, וּמֶלֶךְ מַלְכֵי הַמְּלָכִים הַקָּדוֹשׁ בָּרוּךְ הוּא
טָבַע כָּל אָדָם בְּחוֹתָמוֹ שֶׁל אָדָם הָרִאשׁוֹן וְאֵין אֶחָד מֵהֶן דּוֹמֶה לַחֲבֵרוֹ.

לְפִיכָךְ, כָּל אֶחָד וְאֶחָד חַיָּב לוֹמַר בִּשְׁבִילִי נִבְרָא הָעוֹלָם.

Initially, only one human being was created. This is to teach us that one who destroys a single life is considered to have destroyed an entire world, and one who saves a single life is considered to have saved an entire world....

It also communicates the greatness of G-d. For when a person mints many coins from the same mold, all the coins are alike; but G-d mints every person through the mold of the first human, and yet, no two people are alike.

Therefore, every person must say, "The world was created for me."

MISHNAH

The first authoritative work of Jewish law that was codified in writing. The Mishnah contains the oral traditions that were passed down from teacher to student; it supplements, clarifies, and systematizes the commandments of the Torah. Due to the continual persecution of the Jewish people, it became increasingly difficult to guarantee that these traditions would not be forgotten. Rabbi Yehudah Hanassi therefore redacted the Mishnah at the end of the 2nd century. It serves as the foundation for the Talmud.

TEXT 5

RABBI SIMON JACOBSON, *TOWARD A MEANINGFUL LIFE*
(NEW YORK: WILLIAM MORROW, 1995), PP. 14–15

Birth is G-d saying you matter....

Your birth was not an accident; G-d chooses each of us to fulfill a specific mission in this world, just as a composer arranges each musical note. Take away one note, and the entire composition is affected. Each person matters; each person is irreplaceable....

Many people seem to feel that because *we* didn't *choose* to enter the world, our birth is a stroke of coincidence or serendipity. This couldn't be further from the truth. Birth is G-d's way of saying that He has invested His will and energy in creating you; G-d feels great joy when you are born, the greatest pleasure imaginable, for the moment of birth realizes His intention in wanting you.

RABBI SIMON JACOBSON

Author of the best-selling *Toward a Meaningful Life* (New York: William Morrow, 1995), which has been translated into 12 languages, and founder of the Meaningful Life Center, which seeks to bridge the secular and the spiritual. For over 14 years, Rabbi Jacobson headed a team of scholars responsible for publishing the public talks of Rabbi Menachem M. Schneerson, the Lubavitcher Rebbe. He is also the publisher of *The Algemeiner* (formerly *Der Algemeiner Journal*), a New York-based newspaper covering American and international Jewish and Israel-related news.

TEXT 6

RABBI TSADOK HAKOHEN RABINOWITZ, *TSIDKAT HATSADIK* 154

כְּשֵׁם שֶׁצָּרִיךְ אָדָם לְהַאֲמִין בְּהַשֵּׁם בָּרוּךְ יִתְבָּרֵךְ, כַּךְ צָרִיךְ אַחַר כַּךְ לְהַאֲמִין בְּעַצְמוֹ. רְצוֹנִי לוֹמַר, שֶׁיֵּשׁ לְהַשֵּׁם יִתְבָּרֵךְ עֵסֶק עִמּוֹ וְשֶׁאֵינֶנּוּ פּוֹעֵל בָּטֵל... רַק צָרִיךְ לְהַאֲמִין כִּי נַפְשׁוֹ מִמְּקוֹר הַחַיִּים יִתְבָּרֵךְ שְׁמוֹ, וְהַשֵּׁם יִתְבָּרֵךְ מִתְעַנֵּג וּמִשְׁתַּעֲשֵׁעַ בָּהּ כְּשֶׁעוֹשָׂה רְצוֹנוֹ.

Just as we must believe in G-d, so too, we must afterward believe in ourselves—that G-d cares about us, that we are not worthless laborers,... that we possess divine souls, and that G-d takes pleasure and joy when we fulfill His desire.

RABBI TSADOK HAKOHEN RABINOWITZ OF LUBLIN
1823–1900

Chasidic master and thinker. Rabbi Tsadok was born into a Lithuanian rabbinic family and later joined the Chasidic movement. He was a follower of the Chasidic leaders Rabbi Mordechai Yosef Leiner of Izbica and Rabbi Leibel Eiger. He succeeded Rabbi Eiger after his passing and became a rebbe in Lublin, Poland. He authored many works on Jewish law, Chasidism, kabbalah, and ethics, as well as scholarly essays on astronomy, geometry, and algebra.

QUESTION FOR DISCUSSION

How might the aforementioned ideas help us deal with a low self-esteem that stems from comparing oneself to others?

TEXT 7

RABBI YOSEF YITSCHAK SCHNEERSOHN, *IGROT KODESH 7*, P. 320

בְּמַעֲנֶה עַל כְּתָבוֹ; בְּהִתְאוֹנְנוּת עַל אֹדוֹת מַעֲמָדוֹ וּמַצָּבוֹ הָרוּחָנִי, הִנֵּה
בֶּטַח קָרָאתָ אֶת הַשִּׂיחוֹת אֲשֶׁר מִתְּנָאֵי עֲבוֹדָה מְסֻדֶּרֶת - שֶׁלֹּא לְהַכְבִּיד
עַל עַצְמוֹ בְּטַעֲנוֹת וּתְבִיעוֹת בִּלְתִּי מְיוּסָּדוֹת, כִּי הָרוֹצֶה לְתַקֵּן עַצְמוֹ הִנֵּה
כְּשֵׁם שֶׁצָּרִיךְ לָדַעַת אֶת חֶסְרוֹנוֹת עַצְמוֹ, כֵּן צָרִיךְ לָדַעַת מַעֲלַת עַצְמוֹ,
כִּי בִּשְׁבִיל עֲבוֹדָה צְרִיכִים שֶׁיִּהְיֶה אַ גוּטֶע שְׁטִימוּנג וְלֹא לְהַשְׁפִּיל עַצְמוֹ
תָּמִיד...

יֵשׁ לוֹ כַּמָּה עִנְיָנִים, הֵן מֵעִנְיְנֵי לִימוּד וְהֵן מֵעִנְיְנֵי הַנְהָגָה מַה שֶּׁבְּעֶזְרַת
הַשֵּׁם יִתְבָּרֵךְ יְכוֹלִים לְשַׂמֵּחַ אֶת לְבָבוֹ וְלָתֵת לוֹ כֹּחַ וְעֹוז לַעֲבֹד עֲבוֹדָתוֹ.

In response to your letter with your complaints about your spiritual status.

I assume you read my talks in which I explained that a condition for orderly spiritual growth is to avoid burdening yourself with foundationless accusations and claims. If you desire to improve, then just as you need to know your shortcomings, so you must know your personal strengths. This is important, because spiritual growth hinges on a positive mood, not on constant self-degradation....

You have a number of things, both in terms of your studies as well as your actions, that should make you happy about yourself. Knowing these will give you the power to pursue spiritual growth.

TEXT 8

THE REBBE, RABBI MENACHEM MENDEL SCHNEERSON,
TORAT MENACHEM 5742:1, PP. 52-53

וּכְיָדוּעַ פִּתְגָּם רַבּוֹתֵינוּ נְשִׂיאֵינוּ (לִיקוּטֵי דִּיבּוּרִים ח"ד, תקפא, א):

"כְּשֵׁם שֶׁצְּרִיכִים לֵידַע אֶת הַחֶסְרוֹנוֹת, כְּמוֹ כֵן צְרִיכִים לֵידַע
מַעֲלוֹת עַצְמוֹ".

וּבָזֶה יֶשְׁנוֹ דִיוּק נִפְלָא: כַּאֲשֶׁר מְדוּבָּר אוֹדוֹת הַמַּעֲלוֹת, הַלָּשׁוֹן הוּא מַעֲלוֹת עַצְמוֹ, וְאִילוּ כַּאֲשֶׁר מְדוּבָּר אוֹדוֹת הַחֶסְרוֹנוֹת, הַלָּשׁוֹן הוּא חֶסְרוֹנוֹת סְתָּם וְלֹא חֶסְרוֹנוֹת עַצְמוֹ.

וְהַבִּיאוּר בָּזֶה עַל פִּי מַה שֶׁכָּתוּב בַּזֹהַר (ח"ג יג, ב): "וְנֶפֶשׁ כִּי תֶחֱטָא (וַיִּקְרָא ד, ב)—תְּוָוהָא".

יְהוּדִי מִצַּד עַצְמוֹ אֵינוֹ שַׁיָּיךְ לְעִנְיָן שֶׁל חֵטְא כְּלָל. וְגַם כַּאֲשֶׁר נִכְשַׁל בְּעִנְיָן שֶׁל חֵטְא חַס וְשָׁלוֹם, אֵין זֶה חִסָּרוֹן עַצְמוֹ אֶלָּא זֶהוּ דָבָר שֶׁמְּחוּץ הֵימֶנּוּ שֶׁנִּדְבַּק אֵלָיו. זֹאת אוֹמֶרֶת: הֱיוֹת שֶׁהוּא נִמְצָא בָּעוֹלָם הַזֶּה הַגַּשְׁמִי וְהַחוּמְרִי . . . יִתָּכֵן שֶׁנִּדְבַּק אֶצְלוֹ מַשֶּׁהוּ מִגַּשְׁמִיּוּת וְחוּמְרִיּוּת הָעוֹלָם. וְלָכֵן אַף עַל פִּי שֶׁזֶּהוּ חִסָּרוֹן, אֵין זֶה חִסָּרוֹן עַצְמוֹ, כִּי חִסָּרוֹן זֶה אֵינוֹ מִצַּד עַצְמוֹ אֶלָּא מִצַּד מְצִיאוּת הָעוֹלָם שֶׁמִּסְבִיבוֹ.

RABBI MENACHEM MENDEL SCHNEERSON
1902–1994

The towering Jewish leader of the 20th century, known as "the Lubavitcher Rebbe," or simply as "the Rebbe." Born in southern Ukraine, the Rebbe escaped Nazi-occupied Europe, arriving in the U.S. in June 1941. The Rebbe inspired and guided the revival of traditional Judaism after the European devastation, impacting virtually every Jewish community the world over. The Rebbe often emphasized that the performance of just one additional good deed could usher in the era of Mashiach. The Rebbe's scholarly talks and writings have been printed in more than 200 volumes.

There is a well-known teaching of the rebbes of Chabad:

"Just as we need to know the defects, so too, we need to know our strengths."

The anomaly in this phrase is that it says "*our* strengths," but with regard to defects it merely says, "*the* defects," not "*our* defects." What is the reason for this?

Leviticus 4:2 states, "When a soul sins" [and discusses the process of rectification]. The *Zohar* (3:13b), however, phrases this as a question: "A soul sinned? Is that possible?"

Meaning, the concept of sin is completely alien to our being. Even when we stumble, G-d forbid, it does not undermine who we are; rather, it is something outside of our nature that has latched on to us. We are residents of a material and mundane world.... It is therefore possible for something unholy to attach itself to us. Though it is a defect, in a sense, it is not *our* defect, but a defect imposed on us by our environment.

TEXT 9

RABBI SHALOM DOVBER SCHNEERSOHN,
SEFER HAMAAMARIM 5679, P. 91

דְּעֲנָוָה אֵינָהּ הַשִּׁפְלוּת מִצַּד פְּחִיתוּת הַנֶּפֶשׁ, שֶׁאֵינוֹ מוֹצֵא טוֹב בְּעַצְמוֹ, אוֹ שֶׁחַס וְשָׁלוֹם הוּא בְּדֶרֶךְ לֹא טוֹב.

כִּי אִם הַשִּׁפְלוּת דְּעֲנָוָה הוּא מִצַּד הֶעְדֵּר הֶרְגֵּשׁ עַצְמוֹ, שֶׁאֵינוֹ מְחַשֵּׁב אֶת עַצְמוֹ לִמְצִיאוּת גַּם בְּכָל הַטּוֹב שֶׁלּוֹ. דְעִם הֱיוֹתוֹ טוֹב וְיָשָׁר בַּתּוֹרָה וּמִצְוֹת וּבַעֲבוֹדָה בִּמְסִירוּת נֶפֶשׁ, אֵינוֹ בַּחֲשִׁיבוּת בְּעַצְמוֹ לִהְיוֹת בְּעֵינָיו בְּאֵיזֶה מַעֲלָה וּמַדְרֵגָא מִשּׁוּם זֶה. אֵין זֶה שֶׁאֵינוֹ יוֹדֵעַ מֵהַטּוֹב שֶׁלּוֹ, כִּי אִם יוֹדֵעַ הוּא שֶׁהוּא טוֹב וְיָשָׁר בְּכָל דָּבָר, וּמִכָּל מָקוֹם, אֵינוֹ מַחֲזִיק טִיבוּתָא לְנַפְשֵׁיהּ שֶׁהוּא בְּאֵיזֶה מַעֲלָה וּמַדְרֵגָא כו'. וְסִיבַּת הַדָּבָר הוּא מִפְּנֵי הַבִּטוּל בְּעֶצֶם.

RABBI SHALOM DOVBER SCHNEERSOHN
(RASHAB) 1860–1920

Chasidic rebbe. Rabbi Shalom Dovber became the 5th leader of the Chabad movement upon the passing of his father, Rabbi Shmuel Schneersohn. He established the Lubavitch network of *yeshivot* called Tomchei Temimim. He authored many volumes of Chasidic discourses and is renowned for his lucid and thorough explanations of kabbalistic concepts.

Humility is not synonymous with feelings of inferiority, or with not finding within yourself any good, or with thinking that you are on a bad path, G-d forbid.

To have humility means to not sense yourself.

Although you are good and on the correct path in matters of Torah and *mitzvot*, and although you are committed to serving G-d with great self-sacrifice, nevertheless, you do not self-aggrandize or think that you have reached some unique level. It is not that you do not know about your good; it's that you don't claim credit or think that you have earned special standing.

And this results from being completely unabsorbed in yourself.

TEXT 10

RABBI YOSEF YITSCHAK SCHNEERSOHN,
SEFER HAMAAMARIM 5701, P. 49

וּכְמוֹ בְּמִי שֶׁמַּרְגִּישׁ בְּרֹאשׁוֹ אוֹ בְּאֶחָד מֵאֵבָרָיו, הִנֵּה הֶרְגֵּשׁ זֶה עַצְמוֹ הוּא הוֹרָאָה עַל הַחוֹלִי. דְּמִי שֶׁהוּא בָּרִיא אֵינוֹ מַרְגִּישׁ אֶת אֵבָרָיו.

וְכֵן הוּא בְּרוּחָנִיּוּת, דְּמִי שֶׁהוּא מַרְגִּישׁ אֶת עַצְמוֹ, דְּזֶהוּ גַּסּוּת הָרוּחַ וְגַאֲוָה, הֲרֵי הֶרְגֵּשׁ זֶה הוֹרָאָה עַל חוֹלִי הַנֶּפֶשׁ. דְּמִי שֶׁהוּא בָּרִיא בְּנַפְשׁוֹ הֲרֵי אֵינוֹ מַרְגִּישׁ אֶת עַצְמוֹ.

If you are feeling your head or one of your limbs, it indicates illness. Healthy people do not feel their limbs.

The same applies in the spiritual sense: if you are feeling your own existence, it indicates an illness of character, namely, arrogance. Those who are spiritually healthy do not feel themselves.

TEXT 11

VIKTOR FRANKL, *THE UNHEARD CRY FOR MEANING: PSYCHOTHERAPY AND HUMANISM* (NEW YORK: SIMON AND SCHUSTER, 1978), PP. 31–35

The will to meaning is not only a matter of faith but also a fact. Since I introduced the concept in 1949, it has been empirically corroborated and validated by several authors, using tests and statistics.... The will to meaning is not only a true manifestation of man's humanness, but also ... a reliable criterion of mental health....

I thereby understand the primordial anthropological fact that being human is being always directed, and pointing, to something or someone other than oneself: to a meaning to fulfill or another human being to encounter, a cause to serve or a person to love. Only to the extent that someone is living out this self-transcendence of human existence, is he truly human or does he become his true self. He becomes so, not by concerning himself with his self's actualization, but by forgetting himself and giving himself, overlooking himself and focusing outward.

Consider the eye, an analogy I am fond of invoking. When, apart from looking in a mirror, does the eye see anything of itself? An eye with a cataract may see something like a cloud, which is its cataract; an eye with glaucoma may see its glaucoma as a rainbow halo around the lights. A healthy eye sees nothing of itself—it is self-transcendent.

What is called self-actualization is, and must remain, the unintended effect of self-transcendence; it is ruinous and self-defeating to make it the target.

VIKTOR EMIL FRANKL
1905–1997

M.D., PhD, founder of logotherapy. Frankl was professor of neurology and psychiatry at the University of Vienna Medical School. During World War II, he spent 3 years in various concentration camps, including Theresienstadt, Auschwitz, and Dachau. Frankl was the founder of the psychotherapeutic school called logotherapy. Frankl authored 39 books, which have been published in 38 languages. His most famous book, *Man's Search for Meaning*, has sold over 9 million copies in the U.S. alone.

Exercise 2.3

1   Which idea from this lesson would be most helpful for you to enhance and reinforce a healthy self-concept?

2   In what way can I grow in this regard?

3   What will be most difficult about doing so?

4   What will be the benefits of doing so?

Key Points

1. The way we perceive ourselves is crucial to our emotional well-being. A negative self-image or feeling dispensable can impede our happiness.

2. The Torah's Creation narrative conveys that the human being is created in the divine image, in order to partner with G-d to advance civilization and make the world a more G-dly place. Every individual is indispensable for this project, as each person has a specific task that only he or she can fulfill. Thus, birth is G-d saying you matter.

3. When we internalize the messages from the Torah about the human being, we emerge with a G-d-based, well-grounded perception of ourselves as important and indispensable. We are also empowered to cease comparing ourselves to others and their accomplishments.

4. When we find ourselves focusing on our flaws, we need to ensure that our assessment is accurate. This includes remembering that just as we need to know our shortcomings, so we must know our strengths. Indeed, we often need a mentor or good friend to help us gain a balanced self-concept. When engaged in an accurate assessment, we will surely find many merits and redeeming qualities that lead us to take a positive view of ourselves.

5 While we should not overlook our faults, we also should not define ourselves by them. Judaism empowers us to define ourselves (and others) exclusively by who we are: beings created in the divine image, who share an unbreakable bond with G-d, tasked with a specific mission that only we can execute.

6 True humility provides us with a self-concept that is conducive to happiness. Humility is not a distortion of the truth, it is not a negative self-image, and it does not ensue from our shortcomings and failures. Humility means that our concept of self slips below the threshold of awareness, as we are completely focused on fulfilling life's calling. This insulates us from self-doubt and thus helps us cultivate a healthy self-concept.

7 Because we are purposeful beings, we find happiness when we are true to who we are—completely focused on our purpose.

Appendix

TEXT 12

MIDRASH, *BEREISHIT RABAH* 16:3

אוֹמְרִים לִפְרָת: לָמָה אֵין קוֹלֶךְ הוֹלֵךְ? אָמַר לָהֶם: אֵינִי צָרִיךְ. מַעֲשַׂי
מוֹדִיעִים אוֹתִי. אָדָם נוֹטֵעַ בִּי נְטִיעָה וְהִיא עוֹשָׂה לִשְׁלֹשִׁים יוֹם. זוֹרֵעַ בִּי
יֶרֶק וְהִיא עוֹמֶדֶת לג׳ יָמִים.

אוֹמְרִים לְחִדֶּקֶל: לָמָה קוֹלֶךְ הוֹלֵךְ?

אָמַר לָהֶם: הַלְוַאי נִשְׁמַע קוֹלִי וְנֵרָאֶה.

They say to the Euphrates River, "Why is your sound not audible?"

"My deeds make me known," it replied. "When a person plants a plant next to me, it matures in thirty days; when a person sows a vegetable next to me, it sprouts in three days."

They say to the Tigris River, "Why is your sound audible?"

"If only my voice would be heard so that I may be noticed," it answered.

BEREISHIT RABAH

An early rabbinic commentary on the Book of Genesis. This Midrash bears the name of Rabbi Oshiya Rabah (Rabbi Oshiya "the Great"), whose teaching opens this work. This Midrash provides textual exegeses and stories, expounds upon the biblical narrative, and develops and illustrates moral principles. Produced by the sages of the Talmud in the Land of Israel, its use of Aramaic closely resembles that of the Jerusalem Talmud. It was first printed in Constantinople in 1512 together with 4 other Midrashic works on the other 4 books of the Pentateuch.

TEXT 13

RABBI YISRAEL BAAL SHEM TOV, *KETER SHEM TOV* 145

שֶׁרוֹב עַנְוְתָנוּתוֹ שֶׁל הָאָדָם גּוֹרֵם שֶׁנִּתְרַחֵק מֵעֲבוֹדַת הַשֵּׁם יִתְבָּרֵךְ. שֶׁמַצַּד שִׁפְלוּתוֹ אֵינוֹ מַאֲמִין כִּי הָאָדָם גּוֹרֵם עַל יְדֵי תְּפִלָּתוֹ וְתוֹרָתוֹ שֶׁפַע אֶל כָּל הָעוֹלָמוֹת, וְגַם הַמַּלְאָכִים נִזּוֹנִין עַל יְדֵי תּוֹרָתוֹ וּתְפִלָּתוֹ. שֶׁאִלּוּ הָיָה מַאֲמִין זֶה כַּמָּה הָיָה עוֹבֵד ה׳ בְּשִׂמְחָה וּבְיִרְאָה מֵרוֹב כֹּל . . .

הָאָדָם רָאוּי לָשׂוּם לֵב וְלוֹמַר כִּי הוּא ״סֻלָּם מוּצָב אַרְצָה וְרֹאשׁוֹ מַגִּיעַ הַשָּׁמַיְמָה״ (בְּרֵאשִׁית כח, יב), וְכָל תְּנוּעוֹתָיו וַעֲסָקָיו וְדִבּוּרוֹ וְהִלּוּכוֹ עוֹשֶׂה רוֹשֶׁם לְמַעְלָה.

RABBI YISRAEL BAAL SHEM TOV (BESHT) 1698–1760

Founder of the Chasidic movement. Born in Slutsk, Belarus, the Baal Shem Tov was orphaned as a child. He served as a teacher's assistant and clay digger before founding the Chasidic movement and revolutionizing the Jewish world with his emphasis on prayer, joy, and love for every Jew, regardless of his or her level of Torah knowledge.

Misguided humility distances a person from serving G-d. Our perceived lowliness leads us to disbelieve that our prayers and Torah study stimulate a flow of divine effluence to all the supernal worlds and that the angels are nourished by our Torah study and prayer. On the other hand, if we truly believe that our actions accomplish all this, how incredibly great would be the joy and reverence that accompany our service….

We should be mindful that we are "a ladder that is stood upon earth whose head reaches the heavens" (Genesis 28:12). All our gestures, engagements, words, and movements have an effect on high.

TEXT 14

RABBI SHALOM DOVBER SCHNEERSOHN,
SEFER HAMAAMARIM 5679, P. 92

כַּאֲשֶׁר מִתְבּוֹנֵן שֶׁכָּל הַטּוֹב שֶׁלוֹ אֵינוֹ מִצַּד עַצְמוֹ כִּי אִם בִּירוּשָׁה לָנוּ
מֵאֲבוֹתֵינוּ, וּכְמוֹ מַה שֶׁהוּא מַאֲמִין בַּהּ' וְדָבוּק בֶּאֱלֹקוּת בִּדְבֵיקוּת אַהֲבָה
וְיִרְאָה כו', הֲרֵי הָאֱמוּנָה שֶׁלוֹ אֵינוֹ מִשּׁוּם הַהַכָּרָה שֶׁמַּכִּיר אֱלֹקוּת, רַק
שֶׁהוּא לוֹ בִּירוּשָׁה מֵאַבְרָהָם אָבִינוּ ע"ה, שֶׁהָיָה מַאֲמִין הָרִאשׁוֹן, וְהָיָה
רֹאשׁ לְכָל הַמַּאֲמִינִים, שֶׁאֶצְלוֹ הָיָה הָאֱמוּנָה בִּבְחִינַת הַכָּרָה, שֶׁהִכִּיר אֶת
בּוֹרְאוֹ . . .

וְזֶהוּ שֶׁכָּתוּב (בַּמִּדְבָּר יב, ג) "וְהָאִישׁ מֹשֶׁה עָנָיו מְאֹד מִכָּל הָאָדָם", הֲגַם
שֶׁיָּדַע אֶת הַטּוֹב שֶׁלוֹ וְשֶׁהוּא גָּבוֹהַּ בְּמַעֲלָה מִכָּל אָדָם, וּמִכָּל מָקוֹם הָיָה
עָנָיו מִכָּל אָדָם, וְהוּא מִפְּנֵי שֶׁזֶּהוּ מַה שֶּׁנִּיתַּן לוֹ מִלְמַעְלָה . . . וְאִלּוּ הָיוּ
אֵלּוּ הַכֹּחוֹת אֵצֶל אַחֵר, הָיָה גַם כֵּן בְּמַדְרֵיגָה זוֹ, וְאֶפְשָׁר הָיָה עוֹד מְגַלֶּה
אֶת הַכֹּחוֹת יוֹתֵר. וּמִשּׁוּם זֶה הָיָה עָנָיו מִכֹּל.

We should contemplate how all the good we possess is an inheritance from our ancestors. For example, our belief in G-d and our emotional connection to G-d have not resulted from our own recognition but are a spiritual inheritance from our ancestor Abraham. He was the first believer, and he truly came to his belief through his own recognition....

This is the meaning of the verse (Numbers 12:3), "Moses was exceedingly humble, more than any person on the face of the earth." Moses was cognizant of his own qualities and was aware that his lofty spiritual level was unparalleled; but he was still humble. He recognized that all of these qualities were given to him from Above.... He felt that if another person would be endowed with the same abilities and qualities as he, the other would have equaled his achievements—or perhaps even surpassed them. It was this that led Moses to be the humblest man of all.

TEXT 15

MIHALY CSIKSZENTMIHALYI, *FLOW: THE PSYCHOLOGY OF OPTIMAL EXPERIENCE* (NEW YORK: HARPER & ROW, 1990), PP. 62–64

When an activity is thoroughly engrossing, there is not enough attention left over to allow a person to consider either the past or the future, or any other temporarily irrelevant stimuli.

One item that disappears from awareness deserves special attention, because in normal life we spend so much time thinking about it: our own self....

In flow there is no room for self-scrutiny.... When a climber is making a difficult ascent, he is totally taken up in the mountaineering role. He is 100 percent a climber, or he would not survive. There is no way for anything or anybody to bring into question any other aspect of his self....

The absence of the self from consciousness does not mean that a person in flow has given up the control of his psychic energy, or that she is unaware of what happens in her body or in her mind. In fact the opposite is usually true.... A violinist must be extremely aware of every movement of her fingers, as well as the sound entering her ears, and of the total form of the piece she is playing....

Loss of self-consciousness does not involve a loss of self, and certainly not a loss of consciousness, but rather, only a loss of consciousness *of* the self. What slips below the threshold of awareness is the *concept* of self, the information we use to represent to ourselves who we are. And being able to forget temporarily who we are seems to be very enjoyable.

MIHALY CSIKSZENTMIHALYI, PHD
1934–

Leading expert in positive psychology. Csikszentmihalyi is professor of psychology at Claremont Graduate University where he directs the Quality of Life Research Center. His research interests are in human strengths, such as optimism and creativity. He is the author of the seminal book *Flow: The Psychology of Optimal Experience.*

TEXT 16

THE REBBE, RABBI MENACHEM MENDEL SCHNEERSON,
TORAT MENACHEM 5712:1 (4), PP. 331–332

שֶׁכַּאֲשֶׁר הָאָדָם מִתְבּוֹנֵן שֶׁנִּיתְּנוּ לוֹ יָמִים קְצוּבִים, יָמִים יוּצָּרוּ גוֹ׳, לֹא
פָּחוֹת וְלֹא יוֹתֵר, וּבְכָל יוֹם, בְּכָל שָׁעָה וּבְכָל רֶגַע צָרִיךְ לַעֲבוֹד עֲבוֹדָתוֹ
לְמַלֵּא שְׁלִיחוּתוֹ בְּעָלְמָא דֵין, הֲרֵי הוּא טָרוּד בָּזֶה כָּל כַּךְ עַד שֶׁאֵין לוֹ פְּנַאי
כְּלָל לַחֲשׁוֹב אוֹדוֹת עִנְיָנִים שֶׁל מַדְרֵיגוֹת . . . וּמִזֶּה מוּבָן בְּמִכָּל שֶׁכֵּן וְקַל
וָחוֹמֶר שֶׁלֹא שַׁיָּיךְ אֶצְלוֹ רֶגֶשׁ שֶׁל שְׂבִיעוּת רָצוֹן . . . שֶׁבְּרֶגַע זֶה שֶׁאֵינוֹ
עוֹבֵד עֲבוֹדָתוֹ, מוֹרֵד הוּא בְּמֶלֶךְ מַלְכֵי הַמְּלָכִים הַקָּבָּ״ה בְּכַּךְ שֶׁאֵינוֹ מְמַלֵּא
אֶת שְׁלִיחוּתוֹ . . . וֶוען מֶען פְרֶעגְט אִים וָואס אִיז בַּא דִיר מִיטְן בְּאַרְצְךָ,
זוֹעֶק הוּא (שְׁרַיִּיט עֶר אוֹיס) בְּמַר נַפְשׁוֹ: מַה לִי רָצוֹן, מַה לִי תַּעֲנוּג, מַה
לִי אַהֲבָה, מַה לִי יִרְאָה (וָואס מִיר רָצוֹן, וָואס מִיר תַּעֲנוּג, וָואס מִיר
אַהֲבָה, וָואס מִיר יִרְאָה), כֵּיצַד יָכוֹל לַחֲשׁוֹב עַל עִנְיָנִים שֶׁל מַדְרֵיגוֹת בָּהּ
בְּשָׁעָה שֶׁצָּרִיךְ לַעֲמוֹד עַל הַמִּשְׁמָר שֶׁלֹּא יַעֲבוֹר אֲפִילוּ רֶגַע אֶחָד בְּמַצָּב
שֶׁל מְרִידָה בְּמַלְכוּת ח״ו מִצַּד הַחִסָּרוֹן בְּמִילּוּי הַשְּׁלִיחוּת בְּרֶגַע זֶה.

When we contemplate that we have a limited number of days, and that on each day and during each moment, we must fulfill our mission, we will then be completely preoccupied with our mission to the extent that we will not have time to think about attaining levels.... Certainly, we will not take the time to feel satisfied about our accomplishments ... because a sense of satisfaction means that we are not fulfilling our mission during that moment, and that is tantamount to rebelling against G-d.... Therefore, when you ask such people about their desires, they yell out bitterly, "What desire? What pleasure? What love? What awe? How can we think about such matters when we need to ensure that we don't miss out on even one second of our mission?"

TEXT 17

RABBI SHALOM DOVBER SCHNEERSOHN,
SEFER HAMAAMARIM 5679, P. 92

דְּשִׂמְחַת הָאָדָם הוּא בְּיוֹתֵר בְּמַתָּנָה, מִפְּנֵי שֶׁזֶּהוּ שֶׁלֹּא הִרְוִיחַ וְאֵינוֹ מַגִּיעַ לוֹ, עַל כֵּן הוּא שָׂמֵחַ בָּזֶה.

אֲבָל כַּאֲשֶׁר בָּא עַל שְׂכָרוֹ הֲרֵי אֵינוֹ שַׁיָּךְ שִׂמְחָה כָּל כָּךְ, מֵאַחַר שֶׁזֶּהוּ שֶׁהִרְוִיחַ בְּכֹחוֹ.

וְעַל כֵּן בְּהַרְגָּשַׁת עַצְמוֹ, הֲרֵי הוּא מְחַשֵּׁב אֶת הַטּוֹב וְהַיּוֹשֶׁר שֶׁלּוֹ וְחוֹשֵׁב שֶׁמַּגִּיעַ לוֹ. מִמֵּילָא אֵין הַשִּׂמְחָה גְדוֹלָה בָּזֶה.

מַה שֶּׁאֵין כֵּן בְּעָנָיו, הוּא שִׂמְחָה שְׁלֵמָה וְתָמִיד הוּא בְּשִׂמְחָה, שֶׁהֲרֵי בְּהֶעְדֵּר הַרְגָּשַׁת עַצְמוֹ שֶׁאֵינוֹ מְחַשֵּׁב אֶת עַצְמוֹ, הֲרֵי אֵינוֹ מַגִּיעַ לוֹ כְּלוּם, וְהוּא רַק בְּדֶרֶךְ מַתָּנָה, עַל כֵּן הוּא שָׂמֵחַ מְאוֹד בָּזֶה.

Our happiness is more pronounced when we receive a gift—something that we did not earn and don't deserve. When we work and get paid, we experience less happiness, because we earned what we received.

The result of this is that people who are overly self-aware, who take their goodness and properness very seriously, are prone to think that they deserve everything that they have. Consequently, their happiness from the things they have cannot be complete.

On the other hand, humble people experience constant and complete joy. They are not focused on themselves, so they don't assume that they deserve things. Everything they have is thus regarded as a gift and makes them very happy.

TEXT 18

SONJA LYUBOMIRSKY, *THE HOW OF HAPPINESS*
(NEW YORK: PENGUIN PRESS, 2008), PP. 130–131

There are multiple ways that kindness can make us happier. Surveys of volunteers, for example, show that volunteering is associated with diminished depressive symptoms and enhanced feelings of happiness, self-worth, mastery, and personal control—a "helper's high."…

Consider an unusual study that followed five women volunteers over a three-year period. These five women, all of whom had multiple sclerosis (MS), were chosen to act as peer supporters for sixty-seven other MS patients. They were trained in active and compassionate listening techniques and instructed to call each patient for fifteen minutes once a month. The results show that, over the three years, the peer supporters experienced increased satisfaction, self-efficacy, and feelings of mastery. They reported engaging in more social activities and enduring less depression.

SONJA LYUBOMIRSKY, PHD

Leading expert in positive psychology. Dr. Lyubomirsky is professor of psychology at the University of California, Riverside. Originally from Russia, she received her PhD in social/personality psychology from Stanford University. Her research on the possibility of permanently increasing happiness has been honored with various grants, including a million-dollar grant from the National Institute of Mental Health. She has authored *The How of Happiness* and, more recently, *The Myths of Happiness*.

GOING LOW TO GET HIGH: THE LINK BETWEEN HUMILITY AND HAPPINESS
EXCERPTED FROM A CHASIDIC DISCOURSE BY THE FIFTH REBBE OF CHABAD, RABBI SHALOM DOVBER SCHNEERSOHN

"The humble shall increase their joy in G-d" (Isaiah 29:19). This verste suggests that there is some connection between humility and happiness; it is specifically the humble who rejoice in G-d.

This raises the question: Feeling humble implies a sense of inferiority to others, a low self-esteem, whereas happiness would seem to be associated with the opposing trait of pride and a feeling of self-importance. How, then, can humility be the vehicle for happiness?

The answer is that humility is neither synonymous with inferiority nor the product of a low self-esteem. Feeling humble is neither the result of a failure to find any positive qualities within ourselves, nor are feelings of humility on account of an inward-directed pessimism. Heaven forbid!

Rather, humility means not paying as much attention to ourselves and that we place less emphasis on our own existence. Despite all of their good qualities, humble people do not think of themselves as particularly special. Despite being virtuous and decent people, who uphold Torah and *mitzvot* even to the point of self-sacrifice, the humble do not self-aggrandize or think that they have reached some unique level. It is not that they are unaware of or in denial of their goodness; they know that they are good and that they act properly; they simply do not claim credit for this achievement or think that it has earned them special standing.

The reason for this is that humble people are totally devoid of self-absorption [given their focus on G-d and their mission in life]. When people are unabsorbed in themselves, they don't make a fuss about themselves, or need anyone to celebrate them, because they have lost consciousness of the self. Therefore, there is nothing to prompt them to self-promote.

RABBI SHALOM DOVBER SCHNEERSOHN (RASHAB) (1860–1920)

Chasidic rebbe. Rabbi Shalom Dovber became the 5th leader of the Chabad movement upon the passing of his father, Rabbi Shmuel Schneersohn. He established the Lubavitch network of *yeshivot* called Tomchei Temimim. He authored many volumes of Chasidic discourses and is renowned for his lucid and thorough explanations of kabbalistic concepts.

Additionally, those who are humble contemplate how the good that they have is not self-created, but comes as an inheritance from their ancestors. Take for example the fact that we believe in G-d and have an emotional connection to G-dliness. This is not the result of our own independent spiritual striving to recognize G-d or to achieve consciousness of the Divine; rather, it is an inborn trait inherited from our ancestor Abraham, the first believer. Abraham is the one who came to faith through recognizing G-d on his own, and he passed down this faith to his descendants. Likewise, the connection we have with G-d—the internal, concealed, divine love that we all possess—it, too, is an inheritance from our ancestors, as it says in *Tanya*.

Think of a child who inherits wealth from a parent. The child didn't work for it; the child merely takes that which was prepared by the parent. The same is true of faith and of our emotional connection to G-d: It is an inheritance. It is not by our own doing alone, but an inheritance from our ancestors.

All of this leads to humility: we don't self-aggrandize because whatever we have accomplished is not due to our own work alone.

This explains the verse (Numbers 12:3), "Moses was exceedingly humble, more than any person on the face of the earth." Moses was cognizant of his own qualities and was aware that his lofty spiritual level was unparalleled; yet he was still humble. He recognized that all of these qualities had been given to him from Above, as the verse (Exodus 2:2) describing the moment of Moses's birth says, "She saw that he was good," which is to say that his goodness was innate.

Moses knew that were others endowed with the same abilities and qualities as his, they would have equaled his achievements. In fact, they may have even surpassed them. This led Moses to be the humblest man of all.

It is this humility that is the vehicle for joy.

When people are focused on themselves, their joy cannot be complete. On the contrary, it is a cause for sadness. It is said that the snake is by nature constantly sad, because he descends from the snake

in the Garden of Eden—the Primordial Serpent—
who symbolizes the selfish inclination. This leads
to sadness.

One might think that a stronger self-perception
would mean that one also senses their own inner
goodness more strongly, which should lead to more
joy. Nevertheless, this joy is incomplete, and for
two reasons:

First, focusing excessively on our positive qualities
leads to a sense of entitlement, which causes our joy
to be incomplete. After all, receiving a gift is more
exciting than receiving a wage. We do not work for
a gift, and so we do not deserve it, which is why
receiving the gift is such a cause for joy. But when
we work for a wage, we deserve it, so there is less
reason to be glad upon receiving it. Therefore, when
we are overly self-aware, when we take seriously our
goodness and therefore think that we are entitled
to everything we have—in this there is no great
happiness.

Second, when we have a strong sense of
ourselves, we never seem to have enough. As our
sages have said, "When we have one hundred, we
want to turn it into two hundred; when we have two
hundred, we want to make of it four hundred, so that
we die without ever having realized even half of our
desires." Therefore, our joy will always be partial.
In fact, we will experience sadness over not having
what we think we deserve.

None of this is the case for the humble—they
experience constant and complete joy. Because
of their lack of self-consciousness, they don't self-
aggrandize, and so they don't think they deserve
anything. Everything that they have is a gift, and this
makes them very happy. They always have enough.
Therefore, their joy is complete.

When the humble don't get something, they are
not saddened; they don't think in terms of being
entitled to anything, so why should they be upset?
More generally, their lack of self-perception leads
them to feel that they are not missing anything and
that all is fine. Therefore they don't get upset and can
always be happy.

This is why it is said that Hillel was so very happy
during the Simchat Beit Hasho'evah celebrations of
Sukkot: it was because he was so very humble, and
true humility leads to great joy.

Sefer Hamaamarim 5679, pp. 91–92

THE JOY OF TRANQUILITY

Facing Stress with Mindfulness, Hope, and Purpose

Stress is an impediment to happiness. How can we rise above everyday worries and frustrations, whether they are about the present or future, and retain our *joie de vivre*? The Talmud has some advice for dealing with anxiety, while a Chasidic master proposes a strategy for changing the way we feel by acknowledging the power of the mind over the heart. Finally, we look at the importance of cultivating optimism and trust from the inspiring example of King David and from the perspective of contemporary research.

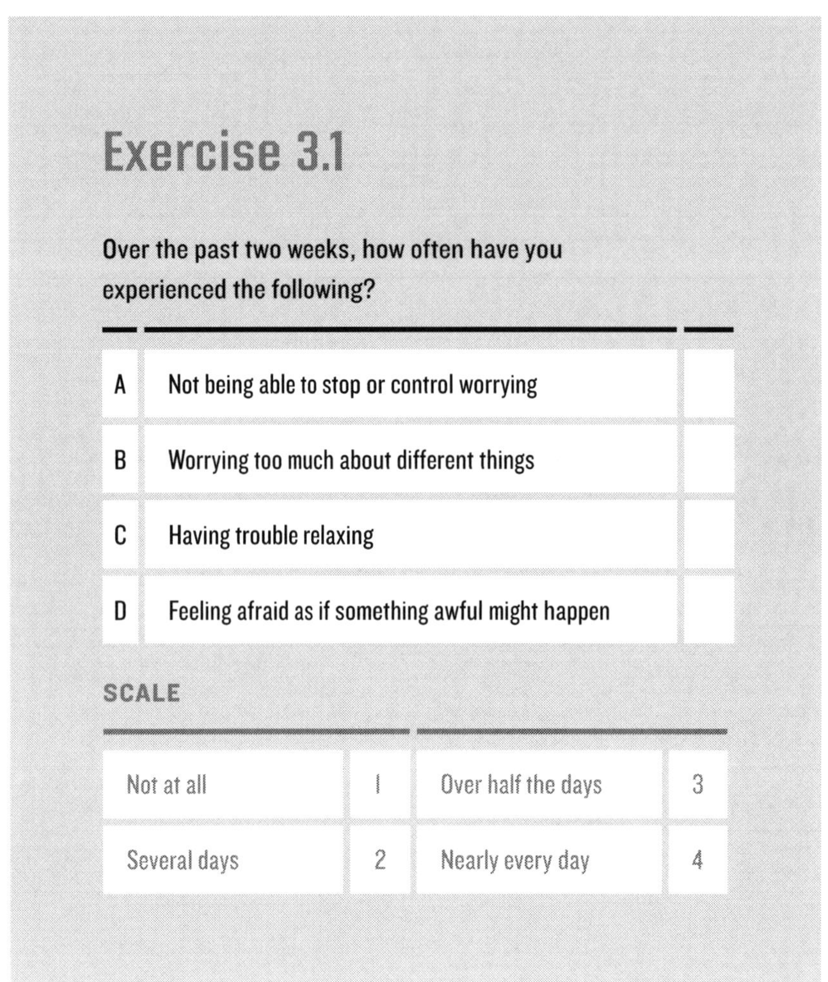

QUESTION FOR DISCUSSION

What strategies have you found effective in managing your worries?

TEXT 1A

PROVERBS 12:25

דְּאָגָה בְלֶב אִישׁ יַשְׁחֶנָּה. ‏

A worry in a person's heart—cast it away.

TEXT 1B

TALMUD, YOMA 75A

> רַבִּי אַמִי וְרַבִּי אַסִי - חַד אָמַר: יַשְׁחֶנָּה מִדַּעְתּוֹ. וְחַד אָמַר: יְשִׂיחֶנָּה
> לַאֲחֵרִים.

Rabbi Ami and Rabbi Asi [interpreted this verse]. One said, "Cast it from the mind." The other said, "Speak about it with others."

QUESTION FOR DISCUSSION

Why does it often help to discuss a worrisome matter with a friend?

TEXT 1C

RABBI YOSEF YITSCHAK SCHNEERSOHN,
CITED IN *HAYOM YOM*, 25 SIVAN

> וּפֵירֵשׁ הַצֶּמַח צֶדֶק: "לַאֲחֵרִים" רַק בְּגוּף, אֲבָל מְאוּחָדִים אִתּוֹ עִמּוֹ,
> שֶׁמַּרְגִּישִׁים אֶת עִנְיָנוֹ.

The third rebbe of Chabad explained: They are "others" only in the bodily sense. However, they are completely united with you, for they empathize with you.

TEXT 2A

RABBI MENACHEM MENDEL OF LUBAVITCH, *IGROT KODESH*, P. 19

עַל דְּבַר מְבוּקָשׁוֹ נִידוֹן הַמּוֹרֶךְ לֵב כו', הֲגַם עַל חִנָּם מַמָּשׁ, לֹא מָנַעְתִּי
מִלִּכְתּוֹב בָּזֶה אֲשֶׁר עִם לְבָבִי.

Regarding your questions concerning fears, etc. Although they are over naught, I have not refrained from answering by sharing what's on my heart.

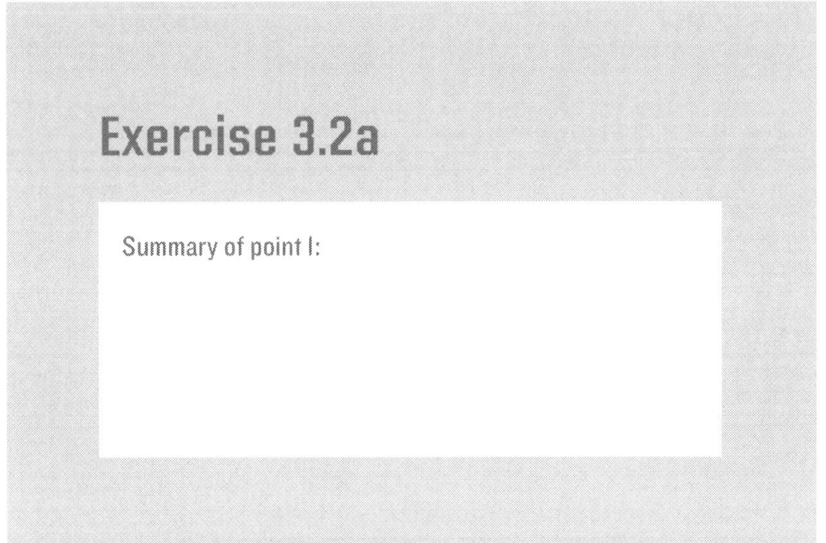

TEXT 2B

RABBI MENACHEM MENDEL OF LUBAVITCH, IBID., PP. 19-20

וַדַּאי שֶׁיֵּשׁ לְבַקֵּשׁ מֵה' עַל שִׂמְחַת הַנֶּפֶשׁ, כְּמַאֲמַר: "שַׂמֵּחַ נֶפֶשׁ עַבְדֶּךָ"
וְכֵן "וְהָסֵר מִמֶּנּוּ יָגוֹן וַאֲנָחָה כו'".

עִם כָּל זֶה יֵשׁ גַּם כֵּן פַּחַד שֶׁהָאָדָם גּוֹרֵם לְעַצְמוֹ, וְהַבְּחִירָה וּרְשׁוּת נְתוּנָה
לוֹ לִמְנוֹעַ עַצְמוֹ מִמֶּנּוּ.

It is certain that you should ask G-d for joy, as it is written, "Cause the soul of your servant to rejoice" (Psalms 86:4). Similarly, we say in our

RABBI MENACHEM MENDEL OF LUBAVITCH
(TSEMACH TSEDEK) 1789-1866

Chasidic rebbe and noted author. The *Tsemach Tsedek* was the third leader of the Chabad Chasidic movement and a noted authority on Jewish law. His numerous works include halachic responsa, Chasidic discourses, and kabbalistic writings. Active in the communal affairs of Russian Jewry, he worked to alleviate the plight of the cantonists, Jewish children kidnapped to serve in the Czar's army. He passed away in Lubavitch, leaving seven sons and two daughters.

prayers, "Remove gloom and lamenting from us." Nevertheless, there are also fears that people trigger themselves, and the choice and authority is given to them to withhold themselves from them.

Exercise 3.2b

Summary of point 2:

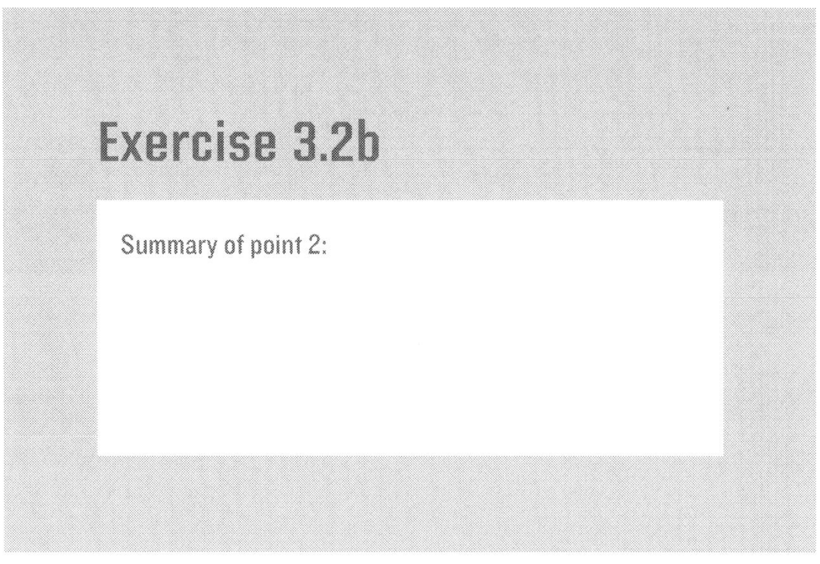

Figure 3.1
First Three Soul Attributes

Chochmah	Wisdom / Creativity	חָכְמָה
Binah	Understanding / Discernment	בִּינָה
Daat	Knowledge / Connection	דַעַת

Machshavah	Thinking	מַחְשָׁבָה
Dibur	Speaking	דִּבּוּר
Maaseh	Doing	מַעֲשֶׂה

TEXT 2C

RABBI MENACHEM MENDEL OF LUBAVITCH, IBID., P. 20

דְּיֵשׁ לְכָל אָדָם ג' לְבוּשֵׁי הַנֶּפֶשׁ, מַחְשָׁבָה דִּבּוּר וּמַעֲשֶׂה, וְהֵם עִיקָּר בְּהַנְהָגַת הָאָדָם, וּבָהֶם הַבְּחִירָה וּרְשׁוּת נְתוּנָה לַחְשׁוֹב וּלְדַבֵּר וְלַעֲשׂוֹת כִּרְצוֹנוֹ בְּמוֹחוֹ. וְאַף אִם מְפַחֵד בְּלִבּוֹ, יוּכַל לְסַלֵּק הַמַּחְשָׁבָה, דִּיבּוּר, וּמַעֲשֶׂה. וְהָעִיקָּר שֶׁלֹּא לַחֲשׁוֹב וּלְדַבֵּר מִזֶּה כְּלָל, אֶלָּא לְצַד הַהֵיפוּךְ . . . וּמִיַּד שֶׁלֹּא יַחֲשׁוֹב בָּזֶה כְּלָל, מִמֵּילָא יִתְבַּטֵּל גַּם הַפַּחַד שֶׁבַּלֵּב. וְעַל כָּל פָּנִים, מִיַּד יִהְיֶה הַפַּחַד כְּאִלּוּ הוּא יָשֵׁן וְאֵינוֹ נִרְגָּשׁ בַּגּוּף. וּבְמֶשֶׁךְ יָמִים אֲחָדִים יִתְבַּטֵּל לְגַמְרֵי עַד שֶׁלֹּא יִפּוֹל בְּמוֹחוֹ כְּלָל . . .

וְהַטַּעַם לָזֶה שֶׁעַל יְדֵי סִילּוּק הַמַּחְשָׁבָה יִתְבַּטֵּל הַפַּחַד הוּא לְפִי שֶׁכָּל הַמִּדּוֹת קִיּוּמָן מֵהַדַּעַת . . . עַל יְדֵי אֶמְצָעוּת הַמַּחְשָׁבָה. וְלָכֵן עַל יְדֵי סִילּוּק הַמַּחְשָׁבָה הֲרֵי זֶה מִמֵּילָא הֶיסֵּחַ הַדַּעַת מֵהַמִּדָּה, וְאָז אֵין הַמִּדָּה מִתְעוֹרֶרֶת . . .

וְהִנֵּה רָאוּי לְמַעֲלָתוֹ לִלְמוֹד אֶת עַצְמוֹ מִכָּל מָרָה שְׁחוֹרָה, שֶׁיֵּשׁ לָאָדָם לְסַלֵּק הַפַּחַד מִלִּבּוֹ, אַף בְּמָקוֹם שֶׁיֵּשׁ מִמַּה לִיפַּחֵד, כְּמוֹ שֶׁכָּתַבְתִּי. וְכָל שֶׁכֵּן בַּנִּדּוֹן דְּמַעֲלָתוֹ, שֶׁבָּרוּךְ הַשֵּׁם אֵין לוֹ מִמַּה לִיפַּחֵד כְּלָל וּכְלָל, בֵּין בִּבְרִיאוּת הַגּוּף וּבֵין בְּמָמוֹנוֹ.

Each person has three soul-garments—thought, speech, and action—that comprise the primary components of human behavior. The choice and power is granted to us to think, speak, and act according to our desire.

Even if you are emotionally afraid, you are able to remove your thought, speech, and action from that emotion.... Immediately upon letting go of the thought, the fear will dissolve on its own. At the very least, the fear will become dormant and will not be felt in your body. And over the course of a few days, it will completely dissipate, to the point that it will not come up in your mind at all....

Removing your thought from the fear will lead to the fear's dissipation because emotions come from the faculty of *daat*... by means of thought. Therefore, by removing your thought, *daat* is automatically removed from the emotion and it will not awaken....

It is appropriate for you to train yourself away from all melancholy. You can remove the fear from your heart, even when there is something legitimate to fear; all the more so in your case, in which, thank G-d, you have nothing to fear at all, whether in matters of your health or finances, etc.

Exercise 3.2c

Summary of point 3:

TEXT 3

FYODOR DOSTOEVSKY, *WINTER NOTES ON SUMMER IMPRESSIONS*
(EVANSTON, IL.: NORTHWESTERN UNIVERSITY PRESS, 1988), P. 49

Try to pose for yourself this task: not to think of a polar bear, and you will see that the cursed thing will come to mind every minute.

TEXT 4

RABBI MENACHEM MENDEL OF LUBAVITCH, IBID., P. 21

> אַךְ עִיקַר הֶיסֵּחַ הַדַּעַת וְהַמַּחֲשָׁבָה הוּא עַל יְדֵי שֶׁיִּשְׁמוֹר מַחֲשַׁבְתּוֹ
> לְהַלְבִּישָׁהּ בְּעִנְיָנִים אֲחֵרִים, דְּהַיְינוּ אֲפִילוּ בְּעִנְיָנִים דְּהַאי עָלְמָא הַנִּצְרָכִים
> וּמְשַׂמְּחִים, וּבְתוֹרַת ה' הַמְשַׂמְּחִים לֵב דְּבַר יוֹם בְּיוֹם בִּקְבִיעוּת עִתִּים
> לְתוֹרָה, וּבִפְרַט עִם עוֹד אֶחָד.

The primary method of removing worrying thoughts from your mind is by directing your mind toward other matters. This can be worldly things, if they are necessary and make you happy. It should also be G-d's Torah—which delights the heart—by establishing fixed times for daily study, particularly with another person.

Russian novelist, essayist, journalist, and philosopher. Dostoyevsky's literary works explore human psychology in the context of the troubled political, social, and spiritual atmosphere of 19th-century Russia. He began writing in his 20s, and his first novel, *Poor Folk,* was published in 1846 when he was 25. His major works include *Crime and Punishment* (1866), *The Idiot* (1869), and *The Brothers Karamazov* (1880).

Exercise 3.2d

Summary of point 4:

TEXT 5

PSALMS 23

מִזְמוֹר לְדָוִד, ה' רֹעִי לֹא אֶחְסָר.

בִּנְאוֹת דֶּשֶׁא יַרְבִּיצֵנִי עַל מֵי מְנֻחוֹת יְנַהֲלֵנִי.

נַפְשִׁי יְשׁוֹבֵב יַנְחֵנִי בְמַעְגְּלֵי צֶדֶק לְמַעַן שְׁמוֹ.

גַּם כִּי אֵלֵךְ בְּגֵיא צַלְמָוֶת לֹא אִירָא רָע כִּי אַתָּה עִמָּדִי שִׁבְטְךָ וּמִשְׁעַנְתֶּךָ הֵמָּה יְנַחֲמֻנִי.

תַּעֲרֹךְ לְפָנַי שֻׁלְחָן נֶגֶד צֹרְרָי דִּשַּׁנְתָּ בַשֶּׁמֶן רֹאשִׁי כּוֹסִי רְוָיָה.

אַךְ טוֹב וָחֶסֶד יִרְדְּפוּנִי כָּל יְמֵי חַיָּי וְשַׁבְתִּי בְּבֵית ה' לְאֹרֶךְ יָמִים.

A song of David. G-d is my shepherd; I shall not want.

He causes me to lie down in green pastures; He leads me beside still waters.

He restores my soul; He leads me in paths of righteousness, bringing honor to His name.

Even when I walk in the valley of death's shadow, I will fear no evil, for You are with me; Your rod and Your staff—they comfort me.

You prepare a feast for me in the presence of my adversaries; You anointed my head with oil; my cup overflows.

May only goodness and kindness pursue me all the days of my life, and I will dwell in the house of G-d for my entire life.

TEXT 6

RABBI BACHYA IBN PAKUDAH, *CHOVOT HALEVAVOT,*
INTRODUCTION TO *SHAAR HABITACHON*

אַךְ תּוֹעֲלוֹת הַבִּטָחוֹן בָּעוֹלָם, מֵהֶן, מֵהֶן - מְנוּחַת הַלֵב מִן הַדְּאָגוֹת הָעוֹלָמִיוֹת...
וְהוּא בְּהַשְׁקֵט וּבְבִטְחָה וּבְשַׁלְוָה בָּעוֹלָם הַזֶה, כְּמוֹ שֶׁכָּתוּב (יִרְמְיָה יז, ז):
"בָּרוּךְ הַגֶּבֶר אֲשֶׁר יִבְטַח בַּה' וְהָיָה ה' מִבְטַחוֹ".

The benefits of trust in G-d include tranquility of the heart in the face
of worldly worries.... The one who has trust finds quiet, security, and
serenity within this world. As it is written, "Blessed are those who trust
in G-d; G-d will be their reassurance" (Jeremiah 17:7).

Exercise 3.3a

Think of someone you trust. Think of what makes them trustworthy in your eyes. Think of them as G-d's messenger, being sent to help you in your life. Think of their presence in your life as a gift from G-d and try to feel that G-d loves you.

Exercise 3.3b

Think of something that you value very dearly in your life (e.g., your hands, your sense of sight, a family member). Think of it as a gift from G-d and try to feel that G-d gave it to you as an act of great love and care. Muster up your appreciation and thank G-d verbally.

Exercise 3.3c

Think of a stressful time when things turned out better than you expected. Think of how you felt before the situation was resolved. Think about G-d's involvement in the situation and what may have occurred had a random force been in control instead. Think of the outcome as a gift from G-d and try to feel G-d's love for you.

Exercise 3.3d

Try to feel trust in G-d the next time you do a basic life activity (e.g., get food from the fridge, turn on/off a light switch, or stand up from your chair).

TEXT 7

DAVID H. ROSMARIN, ET AL., "A RANDOMIZED CONTROLLED EVALUATION OF A SPIRITUALLY INTEGRATED TREATMENT FOR SUBCLINICAL ANXIETY IN THE JEWISH COMMUNITY, DELIVERED VIA THE INTERNET," *JOURNAL OF ANXIETY DISORDERS* 24 (2010), PP. 806–807

Participants in the SIT [Spiritually-Integrated Treatment] group reported significant reductions [in] stress, worry, depression, and intolerance to uncertainty.... Symptom improvement was clinically significant; at pre-treatment, participants in the SIT group reported near-clinical levels of stress and worry ... and at post-treatment and 6–8-week follow-up, reported levels were in the normal range.... The SIT group reported greater treatment gains ... compared to WLC [Wait List Condition] participants. Surprisingly, PMR [Progressive Muscle Relaxation] and WLC participants did not differ on most outcomes....

It is also interesting that Orthodox affiliation was not a predictor of treatment outcomes in the SIT group.... SIT is likely not appropriate for all Jewish individuals. Nevertheless, this surprising finding suggests that interest in SITs among Jews extends beyond the Orthodox community.

DAVID H. ROSMARIN, PHD

Psychologist. Rosmarin is an instructor in the department of psychiatry at Harvard Medical School and director of the Center for Anxiety in Manhattan. He received his PhD in clinical psychology from Bowling Green State University and has written 30 peer-reviewed publications. His research examines the relevance of spiritual and religious issues to psychopathology and its treatment.

TEXT 8

HAVDALAH, OPENING VERSES (FROM ISAIAH 12:2–3)

הִנֵּה אֵ-ל יְשׁוּעָתִי אֶבְטַח וְלֹא אֶפְחָד, כִּי עָזִּי וְזִמְרָת יָ-הּ ה', וַיְהִי לִי לִישׁוּעָה. וּשְׁאַבְתֶּם מַיִם בְּשָׂשׂוֹן מִמַּעַיְנֵי הַיְשׁוּעָה.

Indeed, G-d is my deliverance; I am confident and shall not fear, for G-d is my strength and my praise, and He has been my salvation. You shall draw water with joy from the wellsprings of salvation.

TEXT 9A

PSALMS 37:23

מֵה' מִצְעֲדֵי גֶבֶר כּוֹנָנוּ.

G-d establishes the steps of man.

TEXT 9B

RABBI LEVI YITSCHAK OF BERDITCHEV, CITED
IN *PITGAMIN KADISHIN*, P. 16

יֵדַע הָאָדָם בִּידִיעָה בְּרוּרָה וּצְלוּלָה, שֶׁכָּל נְסִיעוֹת וַהֲלִיכוֹת הָאָדָם לְאֵיזֶה
מְקוֹמוֹת, הַכֹּל לֹא בְּמִקְרֶה הוּא חָלִילָה, רַק מֵאֵת ה' הָיְתָה זֹאת, וּבְהַשְׁגָּחָה
פְּרָטִית. וְכַוָּנַת הַבּוֹרֵא בָּרוּךְ הוּא בָּזֶה, שֶׁיֵּשׁ לוֹ לְאָדָם הַלָּזֶה שׁוּם חֵלֶק מַה
לְתַקֵּן שָׁמָּה בַּמָּקוֹם הַלָּזֶה, הֵן בְּכֹחַ תּוֹרָה וּתְפִלָּה, וְהֵן בְּכֹחַ אֲכִילָה וּשְׁתִיָּה
וְשֵׁינָה לְשֵׁם שָׁמַיִם, וְהֵן בִּשְׁאָר עֲבוֹדוֹת לְשֵׁם שָׁמַיִם . . .

וּכְמוֹ שֶׁאָמַר הַבַּעַל שֵׁם טוֹב זְכוּתוֹ יָגֵן עָלֵינוּ: "מֵה' מִצְעֲדֵי גֶבֶר כּוֹנָנוּ"
(תְּהִלִּים לז, כג), דְּהַיְינוּ שֶׁהַשֵּׁם יִתְבָּרֵךְ עוֹשֶׂה לְהָאָדָם חֵשֶׁק לֵילֵךְ וְלִנְסוֹעַ
לְאֵיזֶה מָקוֹם, וְכַוָּנָתוֹ יִתְבָּרֵךְ הוּא . . . שֶׁיַּעֲשֶׂה שָׁם הָאָדָם הַלָּזֶה אֵיזֶה
עוּבְדָא מֵעֲבוֹדָתוֹ יִתְבָּרֵךְ, כְּדֵי שֶׁיְּתַקֵּן שָׁם הָאָדָם אֵיזֶה תִּיקוּן הַצָּרִיךְ לוֹ,
כַּנִזְכָּר לְעֵיל.

וְעַל כֵּן חַיָּיב הָאָדָם לִרְאוֹת אֶת עַצְמוֹ בִּהְיוֹתוֹ בָּא אֶל אֵיזֶה מָקוֹם לִיתֵּן אֶל
לִבּוֹ מַה זֶה וְעַל מַה זֶה הֵבִיא אוֹתוֹ הַשֵּׁם יִתְבָּרֵךְ לְכַאן, וַדַּאי לֹא לְחִנָּם הוּא.

RABBI LEVI YITSCHAK OF BERDITCHEV
1740–1809

Chasidic rebbe. Rabbi Levi Yitschak
was one of the foremost disciples
of the Magid of Mezeritch and
later went on to serve as rabbi in
Berditchev, Ukraine. His Chasidic
commentary on the Torah,
Kedushat Levi, is a classic that is
popular to this day. He is known
in Jewish history and folklore
for his all-encompassing love,
compassion, and advocacy on
behalf of the Jewish people.

We should clearly recognize that our travels to different places are not
random, G-d forbid, but specifically directed by G-d. G-d's intention is
that a particular person has a specific "portion" to rectify in a particular
place, whether through Torah study and prayer, or through eating,
drinking, and sleeping for the sake of Heaven, or through another means
of serving G-d….

The Baal Shem Tov, of righteous memory, explained the verse "G-d
establishes the steps of man" to mean that G-d imparts the desire to a
person to travel to a specific place with G-d's intention being that the
person should engage there in a particular divine service … thereby
rectifying what this person must rectify.

Therefore, when we come to a particular place, we must take this to heart
and ask ourselves, "Why am I here? For what purpose did G-d bring me
here? It is certainly not for naught."

TEXT 10

THE REBBE, RABBI MENACHEM MENDEL SCHNEERSON,
LIKUTEI SICHOT 23, P. 468 (FEBRUARY 19, 1979)

לְפֶלֶא הָכִי **גָדוֹל** שֶׁלְּאַחֲרֵי שֶׁמְדַבְּרִים וּבַאֲרִיכוּת וְכַמָה וְכַמָה פְּעָמִים עַל דְּבַר תּוֹרַת הַבַּעַל שֵׁם טוֹב (**שֶׁבְּכָל** דָּבָר, הוֹרָאָה בַּעֲבוֹדַת הַשֵּׁם) וְגַם הֵן בְּעַצְמָן **בְּוַדַאי** נוֹאֲמוֹת עַל דָּבָר זֶה, כְּשֶׁקָרָה לָהֶן עִנְיָן שֶׁכַּוָּנָתוֹ **בְּרוּרָה** - **מְחַפְּשׂוֹת** בֵּיאוּרִים מְשׁוּנִים **בְּתַכְלִית** (שֶׁאוּלַי זֶה לְצַעֲרֵן חַס וְשָׁלוֹם, אֵיךְ תַּחְזוֹרְנָה לְבֵיתָן וְכו') **מִלְבַד** הַפֵּירוּשׁ הַפָּשׁוּט:

אֶפְשָׁר הָיָה לְפַרְסֵם הַתּוֹרָה וּמִצְווֹת יוֹתֵר, יוֹתֵר מִשֶׁנַּעֲשָׂה בְּעֵת הַקָאנְוֶוענְשָׁאן, וּמְזַכִּין אוֹתָן עַל יְדֵי שֶׁלֶג הַיוֹרֵד מִן הַשָׁמַיִם, לְהַשְׁלִים הַנַ"ל עַל יְדֵי **שׁוּפִי** (**שֶׁלֹּא כְּרָגִיל**) (עַל דֶּרֶךְ הַשֶׁלֶג) סטָאר'ם בְּיַהֲדוּת וְכו' - בָּעִיר, בִּשְׂדֵה הַתְּעוּפָה, בְּמִכְתְּבֵי-עֵת וְכַיּוֹצֵא בָּזֶה **וְכו'**.

The Baal Shem Tov's teaching that every occurrence contains a directive in serving G-d is a topic that has been spoken of and discussed at length many, many times; I am sure that you, too, have given speeches on this topic. Yet, now, when an incident has happened to you (i.e., your being delayed in Detroit by the N.Y. snowstorm) whose occurrence has a clear meaning and purpose, you seek to attach to the incident most distorted interpretations (e.g., "Perhaps the delay is designed to distress us," G-d forbid, or "How are we going to return home?" etc.)—anything but the simple and obvious interpretation.

The simple and obvious reason for the delay is: It is possible to disseminate Torah and *mitzvos* to a far greater degree than was accomplished during the Convention. You are therefore being granted the merit—through the snow which descends from heaven—of completing the above task with an extraordinary abundance and storm intensity of Judaism, similar to the extraordinary abundance of the snowstorm.

Your efforts in completing the Convention's task of disseminating Torah and *mitzvot* should be extended to the city, the airport, publicity in the newspapers, etc.

Exercise 3.4

Think for a moment about a recent hassle:

1   What did I need out of life at that moment?

2   What was needed of me at that moment?

Exercise 3.5

1   Which of the ideas in this lesson resonated most with you?

2   Which of the concepts would be the most difficult for you
     to implement? Why?

Key Points

1 We are not hostages of our emotions. We can do more than wait out negative emotions.

2 The Talmud presents two approaches for dealing with worrisome thoughts. One approach is to talk over your worries with another person. Another approach is to cast away worrisome thoughts.

3 In most situations, we can govern our emotional lives by controlling our thoughts. Nevertheless, it is often counterproductive to try to stop thinking of something. To cast away a thought, the mind must become absorbed in something else that is relevant and engaging.

4 The basic principles of Jewish monotheistic belief teach us that G-d is benevolent, omnipotent, and caring. This forms the basis of *bitachon*, or trust. We can relax because we are in good hands. "In G-d we trust" helps us cultivate optimism about the future.

5 In one study, believing (but not necessarily religious) Jews, with elevated but subclinical levels of stress and worry, engaged in reflection on the topic of *bitachon* each day for two weeks. They reported significant reductions in stress, worry, depression, and intolerance to uncertainty.

6 One common hindrance to *bitachon* is the feeling that there is no precedent upon which to base this trust. When we stop taking the blessings in our life *for* granted, but *as* granted, we rapidly find robust precedent upon which to build our *bitachon*.

7 Our trust in G-d need not ignore the possibility of future hardship. Rather, "Even when I walk in the valley of darkness, I will fear no evil, for You are with me." While we will likely never understand why G-d allows troubles to occur, we can trust that G-d will be with us—guiding us, supporting us, encouraging us. Knowing this helps us remain calm.

8 The places we go are not random but directed by G-d toward a specific purpose. When we come to a particular place, we should ask ourselves, "For what purpose did G-d bring me here?" This applies just the same for the events of our lives, including those that normally cause us frustration and sadness.

9 Trusting that there is a purpose in every experience—and being determined to discover it and implement it—enables us to remain calm and unafraid when considering the dark moments that may materialize in the future.

10 If we plumb within, we will discover a Divine spark that has passionate faith and unwavering trust in G-d. Bringing trust to our conscious minds is not creating something new but revealing that which is always there.

Appendix

TEXT 11A

MIDRASH, *SHEMOT RABAH* 2:5

מַה הַתְּאוֹמִים הַלָּלוּ, אִם חָשַׁשׁ אֶחָד בְּרֹאשׁוֹ חֲבֵירוֹ מַרְגִּישׁ, כֵּן אָמַר הַקָּדוֹשׁ בָּרוּךְ הוּא כַּבְיָכוֹל (תְּהִלִּים צא, טו) "עִמּוֹ אָנֹכִי בְצָרָה." . . .

אָמַר לוֹ הַקָּדוֹשׁ בָּרוּךְ הוּא לְמֹשֶׁה: אִי אַתָּה מַרְגִּישׁ שֶׁאֲנִי שָׁרוּי בְּצַעַר כְּשֵׁם שֶׁיִּשְׂרָאֵל שְׁרוּיִם בְּצַעַר? הֱוֵי יוֹדֵעַ מִמָּקוֹם שֶׁאֲנִי מְדַבֵּר עִמְּךָ - מִתּוֹךְ הַקּוֹצִים. כַּבְיָכוֹל אֲנִי שׁוּתָּף בְּצַעֲרָן.

In conjoined twins, if one of them feels pain in the head, the other feels it too. Likewise, G-d says, "I am with him in distress" (Psalms 91:15)." . . .

G-d said to Moses, "Don't you realize that I'm in pain just as the Jewish people are in pain? Note the place from where I am talking to you—from the thorns." This is as if to say, "I am a partner to their pain."

TEXT 11B

SIFREI, BEHAALOTECHA 84

כָּל זְמַן שֶׁיִּשְׂרָאֵל מְשׁוּעְבָּדִים, כַּבְיָכוֹל שְׁכִינָה מִשְׁתַּעְבֶּדֶת עִמָּהֶם, שֶׁנֶּאֱמַר . . . "בְּכָל צָרָתָם לוֹ צָר" (יְשַׁעְיָה סג, ט). אֵין לִי אֶלָּא צָרַת צִבּוּר, צָרַת יָחִיד מְנַיִן? תַּלְמוּד לוֹמַר . . . "עִמּוֹ אָנֹכִי בְצָרָה."

Whenever we are enslaved, the G-dly presence is, so to speak, enslaved with us, as it says, . . . "Whenever they have pain, He has pain" (Isaiah 63:9). From this we only know that the G-dly presence suffers with the suffering of the masses; how do we know that this applies when individuals suffer as well? The verse therefore says, ". . . I am with *him* in distress" (Psalms 91:15).

TEXT 12

RABBI YOSEF YITSCHAK SCHNEERSOHN, *SEFER HASICHOT* 5702, PP. 84–85

אַז ר' הֶלֵּל פְלֶעגְט אַרוֹיסְפָאַרן אִין װעג, פְלֶעגְט עֶר מִיטְנֶעמֶען . . . זײַן תַּלְמִיד ר' שָׁלוֹם הוּמֶענֶער . . . פַאַרְנַאכְט-צוּ, זײַנֶען זֵיי אָנְגֶעקוּמֶען אִין אַ אַכְסַנְיָא אִין מָאלָאַרָאסְיָא. ר' שָׁלוֹם הָאט זִיךְ גֶעשְׁטֶעלְט דַאװֶנֶען מַעֲרִיב אוּן הָאט מַאֲרִיךְ גֶעװֶען אִין דַאװֶנֶען בִּיז עֶס אִיז גֶעװָאַרן טָאג. אִיז װִי קֶען מֶען זִיךְ דָאס לֵייגְן שְׁלָאפְן? הָאט ר' שָׁלוֹם זִיךְ גְלײַךְ מֵכִין גֶעװֶען צוּם דַאװֶנֶען בְּעֶרֶךְ אַ שָׁעָה אָדֶער מֶעהר, אוּן הָאט זִיךְ גֶעשְׁטֶעלְט דַאװֶנֶען שַׁחֲרִית, אוּן הָאט אַזוֹי גֶעדַאװֶענְט אַ גַאנְצֶען טָאג. בִּיז אַז עֶר אִיז צוּגֶעקוּמֶען צוּ קְרִיאַת שְׁמַע, שְׁמַע יִשְׂרָאֵל הַוַי' אֱלֵקינוּ וְגוֹ' אִיז שׁוֹין גֶעװֶען מִנְחָה צײַט.

דֶער בַּעַל הָאַכְסַנְיָא, אַ דָאַרְפְס-מַאן, אִיז גֶעקוּמֶען דַאװֶנֶען מִנְחָה. עֶרְשְׁט עֶר דֶערְזֶעהְט װִי ר' שָׁלוֹם הַאלְט עֶרְשְׁט אִין מִיטְן דַאװֶנֶען שַׁחֲרִית. רוּפְט עֶר זִיךְ אָפּ: "װָאס אִיז דָאס מִיט דֶעם אִידְן? נֶעכְטְן הָאט עֶר אָפְּגֶעדַאװֶענְט אַ גַאנְצֶע נַאכְט מַעֲרִיב בִּיז טָאג, אוּן הײַנְט אַ גַאנְצֶען טָאג אַז עֶר דַאװֶענְט. בַּא מִיר אִיז אַנְדֶערְשׁ. אִיךְ קֶען גְלײַךְ זָאגְן שְׁמַע יִשְׂרָאֵל אוּן עֶר אִיז אַזוֹי פִיל מַאֲרִיךְ. עֶס אִיז גָאר פָּשׁוּט, בַּיי אִיהם אִיז אַ פְּרָאסְטֶע קָאפּ!"

ר' שָׁלוֹם הָאט שׁוֹין גֶעהַאט גֶעעֶנְדִיגְט דֶעם דַאװֶנֶען אוּן הָאט זִיךְ צוּגֶעהֶערְט װָאס דֶער דָאַרְפְסמַאן זָאגְט.

הָאט נָאכְדֶעם גֶעזָאגְט ר' הֶלֵּל, אַז דְרַיי יָאהר חֲסִידוּת װָאס ר' שָׁלוֹם הָאט בַּיי אִים גֶעלֶערְנְט הָאט נִיט גֶע'פּוֹעֵל'ט אַזוֹי פִיל װִי דִי װֶערְטֶער פוּן דֶעם דָאַרְפְס-מַאן הָאט גֶע'פּוֹעֵל'ט.

When Reb Hillel used to travel, he would take along … his student, Reb Shalom Huminer.… One evening, they came to an inn in the Ukraine. Reb Shalom began the evening prayer and spent such a long time meditating and praying that morning came. So how can one lie down to sleep? So Reb Shalom set to prepare himself for the morning prayers, taking an hour or more. He then recited the morning prayers, and this took the entire day. By the time he came to the *Shema*, it was already time for the afternoon prayer.

The innkeeper, a simple villager, came to recite the afternoon prayer and saw that Reb Shalom was still in middle of his morning prayers. He cried out, "What is it with this Jew? Last night, he spent the whole night praying, and now he has prayed the whole day! I'm different. I can just say, 'Shema Yisrael,' unlike this man who takes so long. There is only one way to understand this: obviously, this man is a simpleton!"

Reb Shalom had already completed his prayers and heard what the villager had said.

Reb Hillel said afterward, "Three years of studying the teachings of Chasidism with Reb Shalom did not have as much of an effect on him [in terms of self-improvement] as these words of the simple villager."

TEXT 13

RABBI YOSEF YITSCHAK SCHNEERSOHN,
SEFER HASICHOT 5708, P. 235

הָרַב גֶּרְשׁוֹן דּוֹב אִיז אֵיינְמָאל גֶעקוּמֶען אִין לִיוּבַּאוִויטְשׁ אוּן הָאט גֶעוַואַרְט אִין פָּאדֶער-צִימֶער פוּן דֶעם יְחִידוּת-חֶדֶר שֶׁל הוֹד כ"ק אַאַמוּ"ר הרה"ק אוֹיף אַרֵיינְצוּגֵיין אוֹיף יְחִידוּת. דֶערְוַוייל הָאט עֶר זִיךְ אַוֶועקְגֶעשְׁטֶעלְט לֶעבְּן דֶעם אָרְט וואוּ מֶען פְּלֶעגְט אוֹיפְהֵיינְגֶען דִי אוֹיבֶּערְשְׁטֶע קְלֵיידֶער אוּן הָאט זִיךְ פַאַרְטְרַאכְט. מֶענְדְל דֶער מְשָׁרֵת, נִיט וִויסֶענְדִיק וֶוער דָאס אִיז אוּן זֶעהֶענְדִיק אַז עֶר שְׁטֵייט לֶעבְּן דִי קְלֵיידֶער הָאט חוֹשֵׁד גֶעוֶוען אַז עֶר וִויל עֶפֶּעס צוּנֶעמֶען. הָאט עֶר גֶענוּמֶען ר' גֶּרְשׁוֹן דּוֹב'ן אוּן הָאט עֶם צוּגֶעפִירְט צוּ דֶער אַרוֹיסְגַאנְג-טִיר.

הַר' גֶּרְשׁוֹן דּוֹב בָּכָה וְאָמַר . . . "פוּן דֶעם רֶבִּינְס פָּאדֶער-צִימֶער טְרַייבְּט מֶען מִיךְ אַרוֹיס".

Reb Gershon Dov once came to Lubavitch and was waiting in the antechamber for his private audience with the rebbe, Rabbi Shalom Dovber. As he waited, lost in thought, he stood near the place where the

Rebbe's family would hang their overcoats. The attendant, Mendel, not knowing who this was, and seeing that he was standing near the coats, was suspicious that he wanted to steal something. He grabbed Reb Gershon Dov and escorted him out.

Reb Gershon Dov wept and said,…"I've been driven out from the Rebbe's antechamber. [Evidently, I'm not ready for *yechidut*.]"

TEXT 14

THE REBBE, RABBI MENACHEM MENDEL SCHNEERSON,
SICHOT KODESH 5730, VOL 1, P. 470 🔯

סְ'אִיז דָא אַן עִנְיָן וָואס וֶוערט אָנגֶערוּפֿן הַצְלָחָה אִין זְמַן. וָואס הֵייסְט הַצְלָחָה אִין זְמַן? מֶען קֶען דָאךְ נִיט מוֹסִיף זַיין זְמַן אִין דֶעם עִנְיָן פֿון אַרִיכוּת הַיוֹם אָדֶער אַרִיכוּת הַלַיְלָה. אִין זְמַן גוּפָֿא קֶען אָבֶּער זַיין הַצְלָחָה – מֶען זָאל דֶעם זְמַן אוֹיסְנוּצְן אִין דֶעם פֿוּלְסְטָן מָאס אוֹיף וְויפֿל מֶען קֶען אִים אוֹיסְנוּצְן.

דֶערְצוּ דַארְף זַיין אַ הַנְהָגָה אַז מ'זָאל קֶענֶען בַּא זִיךְ פּוֹעֵלְ'ן אַז בִּשְׁעַת מ'טוּט אַיין עִנְיָן, אִיז דִי אַלֶע עִנְיָנִים וָואס מ'הָאט גֶעטָאן פְֿרִיעֶר אוּן וָואס מֶען וֶועט דַארְפֿן טָאן שְׁפֶּעטֶער אִיז כְּאִילוּ אֵינָם בָּעוֹלָם, אוֹיבּ זֵיי זַיינֶען נִיט נוֹגֵעַ צוּ דֶעם עִנְיָן וָואס טוּט אִיצְטֶער.

וְויבַּאלְד אַז עֶר הָאט טַאקֶע נָאר אָט דֶעם רֶגַע קָטָן, אָבֶּער אִין דֶעם רֶגַע קָטָן הָאט עֶר נִיט קֵיינֶע מַחֲשָׁבוֹת הַמְבַלְבְּלוֹת אָדֶער עִנְיָנִים הַמְבַלְבְּלִים, נִיט פֿוּן דֶעם עָבַר, נִיט פֿוּן דֶעם עָתִיד, גִיט דָאס אִים דֶעם מֶעגְלֶעכְקֵייט אַז עֶר זָאל אוֹיסְנִיצְן אָט דֶעם רֶגַע בְּמִילוּאָהּ, אוּן אָט דָאס וֶוערט אָנגֶערוּפֿן הַצְלָחָה אִין זְמַן.

There is a concept called "success in time." What does this mean? We cannot add actual time to the length of the day or night. But within the unalterable constraints of time, we can make the fullest use of it and utilize it to the maximum.

In order to do so, we need to adopt the habit that, when engaged in a particular activity, nothing else exists. Anything that is not pertinent to the matter now at hand, whether it is something that we have previously done or that we need to later do, should be considered as if it does not exist.

All we have is the present moment. But because this moment, brief as it is, will be free of all irrelevant thoughts and matters about the past or future, we will have the ability to fully utilize that moment. This is "success in time."

TEXT 15

MAIMONIDES, *MISHNEH TORAH*, LAWS OF TEMPERAMENTS 3:2–3

צָרִיךְ הָאָדָם שֶׁיְּכַוֵּון לִבּוֹ וְכָל מַעֲשָׂיו כּוּלָם לֵידַע אֶת הַשֵּׁם בָּרוּךְ הוּא בִּלְבָד . . . הַמְהַלֵּךְ בְּדֶרֶךְ זוֹ כָּל יָמָיו עוֹבֵד אֶת ה' תָּמִיד . . .

וְעַל עִנְיָן זֶה צִוּוּ חֲכָמִים וְאָמְרוּ (אָבוֹת ב, יב) "וְכָל מַעֲשֶׂיךָ יִהְיוּ לְשֵׁם שָׁמַיִם", וְהוּא שֶׁאָמַר שְׁלֹמֹה בְּחָכְמָתוֹ (מִשְׁלֵי ג, ו) "בְּכָל דְּרָכֶיךָ דָעֵהוּ".

We should direct our hearts and the totality of our actions to one goal: becoming aware of G-d…. One who always follows this path continually serves G-d….

Our sages instructed us regarding this matter, saying (*Ethics of the Fathers* 2:13), "All your deeds should be for the sake of Heaven." King Solomon, too, declared in his wisdom, "Know Him in all your ways" (Proverbs 3:6).

RABBI MOSHE BEN MAIMON (MAIMONIDES, RAMBAM) 1135–1204

Halachist, philosopher, author, and physician. Maimonides was born in Córdoba, Spain. After the conquest of Córdoba by the Almohads, he fled Spain and eventually settled in Cairo, Egypt. There, he became the leader of the Jewish community and served as court physician to the vizier of Egypt. He is most noted for authoring the *Mishneh Torah*, an encyclopedic arrangement of Jewish law; and for his philosophical work, *Guide for the Perplexed*. His rulings on Jewish law are integral to the formation of halachic consensus.

TEXT 16

THE REBBE, RABBI MENACHEM MENDEL SCHNEERSON, *SEFER HASICHOT* 5751:2, P. 553

בְּשַׁעַת אַ מֶענְטְשׁ פִילְט נִיט דִי כַּוָּונָה וְתַכְלִית אִין זַיין לֶעבְּן (אַז "אֲנִי נִבְרֵאתִי לְשַׁמֵּשׁ אֶת קוֹנִי"), קֶען עֶר נִיט שְׁטֵיין מִיט אַן אֱמֶת'ע מְנוּחָה וְהִתְיַישְׁבוּת, וָוארוּם דִי שִׁינוּיֵי הַזְּמַן וְהַמָּקוֹם אוּן אַלֶע רִיבּוּי פְּרָטִים

וּפְרָטֵי פְּרָטִים פוּן זַיין לֶעבְּן זַיינֶען גוֹרֵם אַ שְׁטֶענְדִיקֶע אוּמְרוּ, וָואס "שְׁפַּאלְט" אִים פַאנַאנְדֶער;

דַוְקָא בְּשַׁעַת עֶר דֶערְהֶערְט דִי צִיל - דִי כַּוָונָה וְתַכְלִית - וָואס לִיגְט בְּתוֹךְ דִי אַלֶע פְּרָטִים, דֶעמוּלְט בְּרֶענְגְט עֶס אִים אַ מְנוּחָה, וָואס אִיז הֶעכֶער פַאר דֶער תְּנוּעָה וְשִׁינוּי פוּן פְּרָטֵי הַחַיִּים, אוּן בְּמֵילָא - צוּ שְׁלֵימוּת הָאָדָם.

When we do not feel the purpose in our lives—that we were created to serve our Maker—we cannot have a true sense of inner peace and tranquility. The continuous changes of time and location, and the myriad details and sub-details within our lives, cause a constant unrest that fragments us in different directions.

When we acknowledge the purpose that lies within all of these details—which transcends the ebb and flow of life's changes and movements—it brings us tranquility and, thereby, human completion.

PATIENCE

RABBI RAPHAEL PELCOVITZ AND DAVID PELCOVITZ, PHD

This chapter will focus on patience facing the daily "hassles" of life as well as patience in the face of long-term challenge. Patience is a trait that is often called for in our daily life. Maintaining one's composure can make the difference between a flourishing or tension-filled marriage, one's ability to parent effectively, and one's effectiveness in getting along with difficult personalities in the workplace.

On a more mundane level, the inevitable frustrations that routinely confront us often challenge our ability to remain calm. A recent poll[1] found that 86 percent of American consumers are put on hold every time they place a call to a business establishment. The time spent on hold by more than half of the respondents added up to thirteen hours a year. That this process tries one's equanimity is documented by the pollsters' finding that 58 percent report that they find the experience of being placed on hold "very frustrating." Developing the capacity for patience can transform the internal experience of being placed on hold, stuck in traffic, or waiting in a long line from one of annoyance and frustration to an opportunity to relax, and welcome the rare opportunity for "downtime."

The far-reaching benefits of patience have been documented in an array of research studies that find higher levels of happiness and more effective overall coping skills in individuals who are patient.[2] In a similar vein, studies have found that minor

RABBI RAPHAEL PELCOVITZ (1921–2018)

Rabbi emeritus, author, and teacher. Rabbi Pelcovitz served as the pulpit rabbi and community leader of Congregation Kneseth Israel (the White Shul) in Far Rockaway, New York, for more than 50 years. He authored a number of books in which he presents ideas from Jewish thought in a compelling and comprehensible way. He also co-authored 2 books with his son, Dr. David Pelcovitz.

DAVID PELCOVITZ, PHD

Psychologist, teacher, and author. Dr. Pelcovitz, who received his PhD from the University of Pennsylvania, has published and lectured extensively on a variety of topics related to education, parenting, and mental health. He is currently the Straus Professor of Psychology and Education at the Azrieli Graduate School, Yeshiva University. His books include *Balanced Parenting* and *Life in the Balance*, both written in collaboration with his father, Rabbi Raphael Pelcovitz.

daily hassles, such as encountering heavy traffic or missing a train, are even more stressful than dealing with major life crises such as a chronic illness or financial difficulties. In one of the first studies that documented this counterintuitive finding, psychologist Allen Kanner and his colleagues[3] found that difficulty dealing with minor daily hassles, such as losing things or feeling time pressure at work, was a better predictor of psychological difficulties than was facing major life events. Similar findings were noted by Dr. Anita DeLongis and colleagues[4] who found that the repeated "minor" annoyances of everyday life were better predictors of health problems, such as headaches or backaches, than more serious major life events. Here too, whether hassles are viewed as a burden or met with patience determines whether life's inevitable minor annoyances will make us ill and unhappy or be faced with equanimity.

Jewish Perspectives on Patience

One of the Thirteen Attributes of Mercy taught to Moshe as the formula for seeking Divine forgiveness is *Erech Apayim*, slow to anger, or patience. We are commanded to "walk in G-d's ways," including nurturing this all-important trait of patience in the face of provocation. The central significance of patience in Jewish life is highlighted by the very first guideline to ethical living recorded in Ethics of the Fathers—the admonition given by the Men of the Great Assembly, the 120 Elders who lived at the beginning of the Second Temple Era:

"Be deliberate (mesunim) in judgment."[5]

This admonition to judges, to show *mesinus*, patience, and caution while they "deliberate" a case, ensures a careful consideration of both sides of an argument in a manner that fairly analyzes all of the evidence. *Mesinus* means taking the time to investigate thoroughly, and allows for compromise as well.

Recent research has documented how essential careful deliberation is to the process of truly understanding interpersonal difficulties. Referring to recent brain research on the need for focus, patience, and "slowness" in being able to truly understand the complexity of interpersonal conflict, Daniel Goleman, the renowned expert on emotional intelligence and social-emotional learning, writes the following:

"While volunteers listened to tales of people subjected to *physical* pain, brain scans revealed that their own brain centers for experiencing such pain lit up instantly. But if the story was about *psychological* suffering, it took relatively longer to activate the higher brain centers involved in empathic concern and compassion. As the research team put it, 'It takes time to tell the psychological and moral dimension of a situation. . . . Where we focus matters: our emotional empathy grows stronger if we attend to the intensity of the pain and lessens as we look away.'"[6]

***

Another facet of patience—*savlanus*—is often used in situations where patience is required over the long term. The word *savlanus* is based on the root "saval" which also means to suffer, or to shoulder a burden. *Saval* is the Hebrew word as well for a porter: an individual who carries luggage. The inner psychological meaning of "carrying luggage" depends on one's perspective. One can view the suitcase as an efficient way of organizing one's belongings while traveling or as "baggage"—a source of suffering, a burden that weighs one down.

A classic example of this is contained in the following beautiful passage from Isaiah, which is recited at the end of the daily *Aleinu* prayer:

> *"Even when you grow old, I will be the same. When your hair turns gray, I will still carry you (esbol). I made you, I will bear you. I will carry (esbol) you, and I will rescue you."*[7]

Here the word *esbol* refers to the concept of *savlanus*: G-d's being there to patiently carry us even in our most advanced years. This is patience over the very long term. It refers to the ability to maintain equanimity even in the face of chronic stress, such as what we face in confronting the inevitable challenges of old age. As Angela Duckworth, a psychologist whose work will be discussed in the next chapter, says in her description of "grit," this refers to the marathon, not the sprint—the ability to maintain one's composure over the long term. As the *Mussar* masters point out, by emulating G-d's infinite patience in "carrying" us in spite of our imperfections and frailties, we, who are commanded to guide our

lives by walking in G-d's ways, should internalize the value of patience both in the short term (*mesinus*) and the long term (*savlanus*). . . .

Torah Perspectives on Growing from Challenge[8]

Developing increased patience with challenges posed by life's setbacks by appreciating their growth-inducing potential is echoed throughout the Torah. The Ramban, in a discussion of Hashem's "testing" Avraham, teaches us a valuable lesson in the Jewish perspective of tribulations:

> *"And Hashem tested Avraham": Hashem tests a person to bring out his or her potential, so that the individual who is tested can earn the reward that comes from a good action rather than that of a good heart alone. . . . All tests that we encounter in the Torah are for the benefit of the individual who is tested.*[9]

This view of the growth potential that is actualized by engaging in the struggles presented by life's ordeals is further elucidated in a *midrash* on this same verse that teaches us about the common etymology of the words *nisayon* (ordeal) and *nes* (miracle or banner) as follows:

> *"And Hashem tested Avraham"*[10] *it is written, "You gave those who fear You a banner (nes) to raise on high, in order to be adorned"*[11] *nisayon (test) after nisayon, i.e., growth after growth, in order to raise them up in the world.*[12]

In a particularly eloquent description of this process we find the following passage in the *Orchos Tzaddikim*:

> *Troubles are for the long-term benefit of the individual. As it says: "Rejoice not against me, my enemy; for when I fall, I will get up; when I sit in darkness, Hashem is a light to me."*[13] *Our Rabbis, of blessed memory, taught us, "If I had not fallen, I would not have picked myself up. If I did not sit in darkness, I would not have seen the light."*[14]

A final thought on developing a patient attitude when dealing with the challenge of having others remain angry with us after we have wronged them and our efforts at apologizing fall on deaf ears. Reflecting a view that a certain amount of suffering in life is inevitable and even beneficial, the *Tomer Devorah*—the 16th-century work of Rabbi Moshe

Cordovero—explains that having others angry at us, because of real or perceived offenses committed by us against them, should be viewed as a blessing. To be "scorned, shamed, or cursed" is viewed as a desirable form of purification, far better than suffering through illness or poverty. As Rabbi Cordovero writes:

> "A person should actually desire these forms of suffering and say to himself. . . . 'It is far better for me to be afflicted with being shamed and scorned by other people, which do not remove my power or weakness.' Thus, when insults are meted out to him, he will rejoice in them, and contrary to the typical reaction, he will desire them . . . and make a balm for his heart."[15]

Instilling Patience in Children

The widely respected research of Dr. Carol Dweck, a Stanford University psychologist, further informs approaches to life's frustrations in a manner that fosters patience and continued effort at self-improvement. Dr. Dweck found, that when faced with challenge, parents and teachers tend to foster one of two mindsets in teaching children how to respond to demanding situations. A fixed mindset is one in which children are taught to believe that whatever talent, abilities, and intelligence they have are innate qualities that exist regardless of how much hard work they put into the task at hand. In contrast, parents and teachers who foster a growth mindset engender a belief in the child that success is about effort and persisting in working hard even in the face of the toughest challenges. A growth mindset is what parents should strive for since children are often energized by challenge, as they demonstrate high levels of patience and the belief that with enough hard work they are up to confronting even the most daunting challenges.

The study that is most often cited as documenting this effect involved fifth-grade students being asked to complete a set of puzzles that were not too challenging for their age.[16] Half the children were told that their performance reflected being "smart," while half were told, "You must have worked hard." When the children were subsequently offered another set of puzzles to complete, 90 percent of the children praised for their effort chose more difficult puzzles. In contrast, most of the children who were told that their intelligence was the reason for their strong performance on the easy set of puzzles chose the less challenging set of puzzles. They avoided challenge to protect themselves from the embarrassment of making mistakes, thereby showing the researchers that they weren't as smart as the researchers thought.

One of the final stages of the study involved giving both groups of children puzzles that were so far beyond their age level and ability that it was virtually impossible for them to correctly assemble them. Again, the two groups approached the task in a totally different manner. Those fifth-graders previously praised for their hard work seemed energized by the challenge. Even though they were unable to successfully assemble the puzzles they persisted longer, showing much higher levels of patience than their peers who were praised for being intelligent. Indeed, the group praised for their "brilliance" gave up much more easily, manifesting high levels of impatience and frustration. In the concluding study, the children who had just faced the frustrating, undoable task were again given the simple puzzles, and the power of the type of praise was now most pronounced. Those children praised for working hard did 30 percent better than the first time they encountered the puzzles, while those praised for being smart showed a 20 percent decrease in their puzzle-assembling performance. . . .

General Interventions to Improve Patience

Patience is thought to manifest itself primarily in three arenas:[17]

1. INTERPERSONAL PATIENCE—This type of patience is evident when our interactions with others often result in frustration. For example, showing patience when teaching someone who is not grasping a basic concept that you find to be self-evident, or dealing with an oppositional child without losing one's cool.
2. PATIENCE IN THE FACE OF MAJOR STRESSFUL LIFE EVENTS—Level of patience demonstrated when facing tough times, such as serious illness, financial crisis, or serious marital conflict.
3. DAILY HASSLES—Patience evidenced in the face of life's minor annoyances, such as long lines at the check-out counter, or being stuck behind a slow driver.

Recommendations for Fostering Patience

The following strategies have been proven to be effective in trying to improve frustration tolerance while increasing one's ability to remain calm in the face of provocation, regardless which of these three arenas are operative:

1. AWARENESS OF TRIGGERS—A first step in increasing one's level of patience is learning how to become more self-aware about what situations or events might be most likely to trigger an angry, impatient response. Specific triggers will differ from person to person. Some might become particularly impatient when faced with individuals whose critical nature reminds them of a family member who they didn't get along with during their childhood. Another might find that situations that are beyond their control, such as a major traffic jam or an unusually long wait at a doctor's office, is particularly exasperating. Systematically tracking one's individual pattern of causes and triggers is a crucial first step. Rabbi Yechiel Perr, of Yeshiva of Far Rockaway, calls nipping impatience in the bud, "opening the space between the match and the fuse."[18] This is similar to Viktor Frankl's description, mentioned earlier in this book, of the space between stimulus and response as the source of our growth. When we become more aware of precipitants of impatience, we are better equipped to occupy the space between the trigger and the fuse of impatience with calming strategies.

2. AFFECT REGULATION AND MINDFULNESS—The ability to regulate emotions such as anger and impatience is based on a number of skills that can, with practice, be learned. A cornerstone of developing the key skills of affect regulation is learning how to be mindful. Mindfulness means moment-to-moment, nonjudgmental awareness that involves developing the ability to learn how to pay attention in a focused manner that avoids "mindlessly" being pulled into anger and impatience. Developing the skill of observing, describing, and fully participating in the moment without judging one's self, others, or the situation is a skill that can be gradually developed.

3. DEVELOPING PATIENCE IN OUR APPROACH TO LEARNING—In *Harvard Magazine*,[19] Professor Jennifer Roberts persuasively argues that the increased pressures and tempo of daily life engendered by technology and the accompanying expectations of constant accessibility and instant responses directly impacts our level of patience. She proposes that one of the antidotes is to develop in ourselves and our children the lost art of paying careful attention to the pace and tempo of learning experiences. In a fascinating essay, she describes an assignment she gives her students that is typically met with resistance and disbelief. The Harvard undergraduates who take her art history class are asked to spend three uninterrupted hours in a museum looking at a single painting while taking notes about what they see. In an age where multitasking often competes with deeper levels of thinking, this assignment provides an experience that helps students better appreciate the difference between *looking* at something and truly *seeing* it. Roberts uses her own experience, spending three hours studying the John Singleton Copley painting *Boy with a Flying Squirrel*. She explains: "It took me 21 minutes before I registered the fact that the fingers holding the chain exactly span the diameter of the water glass beneath them. It took a good 45 minutes before I realized that the seemingly random folds and wrinkles in the background curtain are actually perfect copies of the shapes of the boy's ear and eye—as if Copley had imagined those sensory organs distributing or imprinting themselves on the surface behind him." Roberts concludes that teaching patience, by helping students slow down, focus deeply, and mindfully nurture their ability to develop the skill for deeper attention and thought is a crucial skill for today's students.

In a recent talk I (DP) gave to parents of yeshivah students in Chicago, the audience was surveyed about what they considered to be the greatest challenge to their ability to educate their children in a manner that fostered a meaningful connection to Judaism. The number one challenge chosen by parents was that their children were growing up in a world that lacked "stillness"; i.e., their children's spiritual connections were being hampered by a pervasive state of distraction caused by continuous connection to the world of texting, social media and multitasking. The Baal Shem Tov was said to interpret the phrase *"v'avaditem m'heirah"* in the daily prayer of *"Shema"* as, "get rid of the feeling of being hurried in your life."

Roberts argues that the cognitive and emotional changes brought on by the digital revolution require educators to teach patience as a core social-emotional skill necessary for in-depth learning. If recent research in neuroscience documents that brains of digital natives are being rewired in a manner that can lead to shallow rather than deep thinking, then parents and teachers need to develop a set of tools that include what Roberts describes as "the deliberate engagement of delay."

Some specific strategies for bringing such an approach to the classroom, which, in turn, might also inform our pacing was described by Bauerline[20] who recommends that teachers carve out time in their day for children to read with an unbroken and unbothered focus, similar to that described by Roberts. This approach includes setting aside a time for "slow reading" following these recommendations:

a   Promote a willingness to pause and probe while helping the student develop enough patience to ponder a single sentence for a few minutes: "to insert a hesitant question before moving on."

b   Develop the capacity for uninterrupted thinking. If one pauses in the middle of deep reading to check texts or e-mail they "lose their place in the argument."

c   Foster receptivity to deep thinking—provide space to understand and reflect before agreeing or arguing.

4.   FOSTERING A SENSE OF EMPATHY AND PERSPECTIVE-TAKING—It is easier to be patient when we are able to see things through the eyes of those who are provoking us. When difficult people at home or work upset us, empathy for the underlying causes of their behavior can be very calming. Having an attitude of curiosity about why a family member who is being difficult is acting in a certain manner can lead to improved frustration tolerance. For example, in the case of parenting, reminding yourself that your child's irritability may be related to stress in school or on the playground can lead to greater understanding and lower

levels of emotionalism. In general, an impatient response to the provocations of others is almost guaranteed to fuel more resistance and difficult behavior from the other party. When one deals with interpersonal provocations with criticism or yelling, a vicious cycle can be created that will try even the most patient individual's ability to remain calm. When one reflects back calmness and empathy in a manner that allows the person who is the source of your impatience to feel understood, a de-escalation of the mutual tensions will feed a far less upsetting interaction.

Psychologist Dr. John Krug beautifully illustrates this concept with the following story:

Imagine yourself on a crowded elevator in midtown Manhattan at the height of rush hour. You're going up to the 50th floor, but you become increasingly irritated as the man behind you, in his impatience to get off at his floor, is crowding your personal space by jamming into your back. You find yourself increasingly upset and decide that you are going to give him a piece of your mind when he finally gets off the elevator. When the elevator reaches his floor and he makes his way to get off, you see that this man is blind. What you thought was an inconsiderate individual, rudely jockeying for a good position to quickly leave the elevator, was, in fact, a blind man with a cane trying to steady himself to meet the challenge of keeping his balance.

What effect does the knowledge that this man is blind have on your feelings of impatience? Your righteous indignation gives way to empathy. Your anger and sense of irritation yields to guilt about unfair judgment. Developing the ability to view situations through the eyes of others is often one of the most effective ingredients nourishing the ability to be patient.

CONCLUSION

Developing the ability to remain patient in face of life's inevitable stress is a skill that can have major impact on one's relationships, health, and overall happiness. By working on changing one's perspective when faced either with the "little" annoyances of daily routine as well as when struggling to cope with more major life events, an individual can transform his life into one where frustration can serve as a source of growth rather than as a source of conflict.

Life in the Balance: Torah Perspectives on Positive Psychology *(New York: Shaar Press, 2014), pp. 177–199*

Reprinted with permission of the authors

Endnotes

1. *Time Magazine,* (January 24th, 2013) Business and Money Section, Poll completed by Talk to Text Message Service.

2. Schnitker, S.A., & Emmons, R.A. (2007). Patience as a virtue: Religious and psychological perspectives. *Research in the Social Scientific Study of Religion*, 18, 177–207.

3. Kanner, A., Coyne, J. & Schaefer, C. (1981). Comparison of two modes of stress measurement: Daily hassles and uplifts versus major life events. *Journal of Behavioral Medicine*, 4, 1–39.

4. Delongis, A. Coyne, J. & Dakof, G. (1982). Relationship of daily hassles, uplifts, and major life events to health status. *Health Psychology*, 1, 119–136.

5. *Ethics of the Fathers (Pirkei Avos)* 1:1.

6. Goleman, D. (2013). *Focus*, New York: HarperCollins, p. 107.

7. *Isaiah* 46:4.

8. Based on Pelcovitz, D. (2002). Helping children, adolescents, as well as adults, to cope with loss and terror: Jewish and psychological perspectives. New York State Project Liberty.

9. *Ramban, Genesis* 22:1.

10. Genesis 22:1.

11. Psalms 60:6.

12. Midrash Rabbah, 55:1.

13. Micah 7:8.

14. *The Ways of the Righteous (Orchos Tzaddikim) Shaar HaTeshuvah, Gate 26.*

15. *Tomer Devorah* (2005). Translated by Fink, D. & Finkelman, S. Jerusalem, Israel: Tomer Publications, page 40.

16. Mueller, C. & Dweck, C. (1998). Praise for intelligence can undermine children's motivation and performance. *Journal of Personality and Social Psychology*, 75, 33–52.

17. Schnitker, S. (2012). An examination of patience and well-being. *The Journal of Positive Psychology*, 7, 263–280.

18. Morinis, A. (2007). *Everyday Holiness*, Boston, MA.: Trumpeter Press, p. 58.

19. Roberts, J. (2013). The power of patience. *Harvard Magazine*, 40–41.

20. Bauerline, M. (2011), Too dumb for complex texts? *Educational Leadership*, 68, 28–32.

THE JOY FROM OTHERS

Investing in Healthy Relationships

Compelling psychological research has demonstrated the many remarkable effects of friendship on happiness and emotional well-being. We are inescapably social beings. And yet, both social science and personal experience show that loneliness, disconnection, and division are stubborn realities of life. How can we arrest this disconcerting drift apart? This class analyzes how to mitigate some of the major impediments to our interpersonal relationships—namely, cynicism, disagreement, and an inability to listen to others. It also addresses how to retain equilibrium even during those troubling moments when a relationship causes pain rather than gain.

Exercise 4.1

Take a moment to think of a close and trusting relationship in your life. What would be lacking if this relationship weren't so close and trusting?

TEXT 1

טוֹבִים הַשְּׁנַיִם מִן הָאֶחָד אֲשֶׁר יֵשׁ לָהֶם שָׂכָר טוֹב בַּעֲמָלָם. כִּי אִם יִפֹּלוּ
הָאֶחָד יָקִים אֶת חֲבֵרוֹ, וְאִילוֹ הָאֶחָד שֶׁיִּפּוֹל וְאֵין שֵׁנִי לַהֲקִימוֹ.

גַּם אִם יִשְׁכְּבוּ שְׁנַיִם וְחַם לָהֶם וּלְאֶחָד אֵיךְ יֵחָם.

וְאִם יִתְקְפוֹ הָאֶחָד הַשְּׁנַיִם יַעַמְדוּ נֶגְדּוֹ וְהַחוּט הַמְשֻׁלָּשׁ לֹא בִמְהֵרָה יִנָּתֵק.

Two are better than one, since they have good reward for their toil. For if they fall, one will lift the other; but woe to those who fall and have no second one to lift them up.

Moreover, if two lie down, they will have warmth, but how will one have warmth?

If attacked by someone, the two will stand against the attacker; and a three-stranded cord will not quickly be broken.

TEXT 2

הָאָדָם מְדִינִי בְּטֶבַע, וְשֶׁטִּבְעוֹ שֶׁיְּהֵא בְּתוֹךְ חֲבוּרָה, וְאֵינוֹ כִּשְׁאָר בַּעֲלֵי
חַיִּים אֲשֶׁר אֵין לוֹ הֶכְרַח לִהְיוֹת בַּחֲבוּרָה.

The human being is naturally social. The nature of the human being is to be part of a community—unlike the life forms that need not be part of a collective.

RABBI MOSHE BEN MAIMON (MAIMONIDES, RAMBAM) 1135–1204

Halachist, philosopher, author, and physician. Maimonides was born in Córdoba, Spain. After the conquest of Córdoba by the Almohads, he fled Spain and eventually settled in Cairo, Egypt. There, he became the leader of the Jewish community and served as court physician to the vizier of Egypt. He is most noted for authoring the *Mishneh Torah*, an encyclopedic arrangement of Jewish law; and for his philosophical work, *Guide for the Perplexed*. His rulings on Jewish law are integral to the formation of halachic consensus.

Figure 4.1
The Four Kingdoms

Silent (Inanimate)	דּוֹמֵם
Vegetative (Vegetable)	צוֹמֵחַ
Animate (Animal)	חַי
Articulate (Human)	מְדַבֵּר

Exercise 4.2

Answer yes or no to each of the statements:

1	I give lots of compliments and positive remarks to others.	YES / NO
2	I have someone to whom I can tell my most intimate thoughts and feelings.	YES / NO
3	I rarely or never feel lonely.	YES / NO
4	I am careful about making negative remarks to others.	YES / NO
5	I get along well with my co-workers.	YES / NO
6	I can relax and be myself when I am with friends.	YES / NO
7	I mostly trust my family and friends.	YES / NO
8	There are people I very much love and care about.	YES / NO
9	There are people I could call in the middle of the night if I have an emergency.	YES / NO
10	I have fun when I am with other people.	YES / NO

Source: Ed Diener and Robert Biswas-Diener, *Happiness: Unlocking the Mysteries of Psychological Wealth* (Malden, MA: Blackwell Publishing, 2011), pp. 65–66

Exercise 4.3

List some of the character traits that are helpful for friendships and relationships. Then list some of the traits that hinder friendships and relationships.

TRAITS THAT HELP	TRAITS THAT HINDER

TEXT 3

TALMUD, BERACHOT 58A

הוּא הָיָה אוֹמֵר:

אוֹרֵחַ טוֹב מַהוּ אוֹמֵר? כַּמָּה טְרָחוֹת טָרַח בַּעַל הַבַּיִת בִּשְׁבִילִי! כַּמָּה בָּשָׂר הֵבִיא לְפָנַי! כַּמָּה יַיִן הֵבִיא לְפָנַי! כַּמָּה גְלוּסְקָאוֹת הֵבִיא לְפָנַי! וְכָל מַה שֶּׁטָּרַח לֹא טָרַח אֶלָּא בִּשְׁבִילִי!

אֲבָל אוֹרֵחַ רַע מַהוּ אוֹמֵר? מַה טוֹרַח טָרַח בַּעַל הַבַּיִת זֶה? פַּת אַחַת אָכַלְתִּי, חֲתִיכָה אַחַת אָכַלְתִּי, כּוֹס אֶחָד שָׁתִיתִי. כָּל טוֹרַח שֶׁטָּרַח בַּעַל הַבַּיִת זֶה לֹא טָרַח אֶלָּא בִּשְׁבִיל אִשְׁתּוֹ וּבָנָיו . . .

עַל אוֹרֵחַ רַע כְּתִיב, "לָכֵן יְרָאוּהוּ אֲנָשִׁים" (אִיּוֹב לז, כד).

Ben Zoma used to say:

What does a good guest say?

"How much trouble the host took for my sake! How much meat he brought before me! How much wine he brought before me! How many fine rolls he brought before me! And all the trouble that the host took was only for my sake!"

What does a bad guest say?

"What trouble did this host take? I ate one piece of bread. I ate one slice. I drank one cup. Any trouble that this host took was only for his wife and children."…

With regard to a bad guest, it is written, "People therefore fear him" (Job 37:24).

BABYLONIAN TALMUD

A literary work of monumental proportions that draws upon the legal, spiritual, intellectual, ethical, and historical traditions of Judaism. The 37 tractates of the Babylonian Talmud contain the teachings of the Jewish sages from the period after the destruction of the 2nd Temple through the 5th century CE. It has served as the primary vehicle for the transmission of the Oral Law and the education of Jews over the centuries; it is the entry point for all subsequent legal, ethical, and theological Jewish scholarship.

TEXT 4

RABBI MENACHEM MENDEL MORGENSTERN,
EMET VE'EMUNAH (JERUSALEM, 2005), NO. 629, P. 488.

בְּתַנְחוּמָא פַּרְשַׁת פִּנְחָס: כְּשֵׁם שֶׁאֵין פַּרְצוּפֵיהֶן שֶׁל אָדָם שָׁוִין זֶה לָזֶה,
כַּךְ אֵין דַעְתָּם שָׁוִין זֶה לָזֶה.

כְּשֵׁם שֶׁהִנְךָ יָכוֹל לִסְבּוֹל שֶׁפַּרְצוּפוֹ שֶׁל אָדָם אַחֵר אֵינוֹ דוֹמֶה לְשֶׁלְךָ, כַּךְ
תִּסְבּוֹל אִם דֵעוֹתָיו שֶׁל אַחֵר אֵינָן דוֹמוֹת לְדֵעוֹתֶיךָ.

Midrash Tanchuma teaches, "Just as people's faces are different from each other, so their minds are different from each other."

The implication is that just as you tolerate other people who *look* different from you, so you should tolerate others who *think* differently than you.

RABBI MENACHEM MENDEL MORGENSTERN
1787–1859

Chasidic rabbi and leader. Born near Lublin, Poland, Rabbi Menachem Mendel went on to succeed the Chozeh (Seer) of Lublin and Rabbi Simchah Bunim of Peshischa as a Chasidic rebbe in Kotsk. His teachings, some of which are gathered in *Ohel Torah* and *Emet Ve'emunah*, are well known in the Chasidic world for their sharpness.

TEXT 5

JOSEPH TELUSHKIN, *REBBE: THE LIFE AND TEACHINGS OF MENACHEM M. SCHNEERSON, THE MOST INFLUENTIAL RABBI IN MODERN HISTORY* (NEW YORK: HARPERCOLLINS, 2014), P. 134

What further fortified the Rebbe in his affection for those with whom he had differing views was a carefully cultivated consciousness of the areas in which he and his opponents agreed.

To a rabbi who expressed deep disagreement with him over a certain religious issue, the Rebbe noted that even if they disagreed on this matter, there still remained 612 issues on which they could work together—a reminder to the letter's recipient that they were two allies having a disagreement, not two opponents having a feud (the number 612 was of course a figurative reference to the Torah's 613 commandments, minus one). In this instance, he also reminded Rabbi Shmuel Lew, who had ongoing dealings with the same rabbi, "how positive a person this man and his family were, and how they can be forces for good [so] let's look [therefore] for the unifying force."

For Lew, the Rebbe's approach became a general directive for how to conduct his life: "Look always for that which you have in common with the other person and build that up." This was a good way, Lew came to understand, to avoid alienating potential allies and avoid living an existence filled with needless enmity.

RABBI JOSEPH TELUSHKIN
1948–

Rabbi and author. Telushkin received his ordination at Yeshiva University and a Jewish history degree at Columbia University. He has written many popular books about Judaism, including the best-selling *Jewish Literacy*, and *Rebbe*, a biography of the Lubavitcher Rebbe.

TEXT 6

TALMUD, BAVA METSI'A 84A

נָח נַפְשֵׁיהּ דְּרַבִּי שִׁמְעוֹן בֶּן לָקִישׁ וַהֲוָה קָא מִצְטַעֵר רַבִּי יוֹחָנָן בַּתְרֵיהּ
טוּבָא. אָמְרוּ רַבָּנָן, "מַאן לֵיזִיל לְיַתְּבֵיהּ לְדַעְתֵּיהּ? נֵיזִיל רַבִּי אֶלְעָזָר בֶּן
פְּדָת דִּמְחַדְּדִין שְׁמַעְתָּתֵיהּ".

אֲזַל יָתֵיב קַמֵּיהּ. כָּל מִילְתָא דַּהֲוָה אָמַר רַבִּי יוֹחָנָן אָמַר לֵיהּ, "תַּנְיָא
דִּמְסַיְּיעָא לָךְ".

אָמַר, "אַתְּ כְּבַר לָקִישָׁא? בַּר לָקִישָׁא כִּי הֲוָה אֲמֵינָא מִילְתָא הֲוָה מַקְשֵׁי לִי
עֶשְׂרִין וְאַרְבַּע קוּשְׁיָיתָא וּמְפָרְקִינָא לֵיהּ עֶשְׂרִין וְאַרְבְּעָה פְּרוּקֵי, וּמִמֵּילָא
רָוְוחָא שְׁמַעְתָּא. וְאַתְּ אָמְרַתְּ תַּנְיָא דִּמְסַיֵּיעַ לָךְ? אָטוּ לֹא יָדַעְנָא דְּשַׁפִּיר
קָאֲמִינָא?"

הֲוָה קָא אָזִיל וְקָרַע מָאנֵיהּ וְקָא בָּכֵי וְאָמַר, "הֵיכָא אַתְּ בַּר לָקִישָׁא? הֵיכָא
אַתְּ בַּר לָקִישָׁא?" וַהֲוָה קָא צָוַח עַד דְּשַׁף דַּעְתֵּיהּ.

Reish Lakish died and Rabbi Yochanan grieved after him greatly. The rabbis said, "Rabbi Elazar ben Pedat should go to comfort him, for he is a brilliant scholar."

Rabbi Elazar ben Pedat went and sat before Rabbi Yochanan. To every idea Rabbi Yochanan taught, Rabbi Elazar ben Pedat responded, "There is an earlier teaching that supports your opinion."

Rabbi Yochanan said to him, "Are you supposed to be like Reish Lakish? In my discussions with Reish Lakish, whenever I would say something, he would raise twenty-four objections, and I would offer twenty-four responses. As a result of the give and take, the subject was crystalized. You, however, constantly say 'There is an earlier teaching that supports your opinion.' Do I not already know that my ideas are sound?"

Rabbi Yochanan went about and tore his clothes, crying and saying, "Where are you, Reish Lakish? Where are you, Reish Lakish?" He screamed until he lost his sanity.

Exercise 4.5

1   During the coming week, spend some time with someone who disagrees with you. Focus on things that unite the two of you.

2   During the coming week, discuss with another something that you and the other disagree on. Stay focused throughout on deepening your understanding of the given issue.

TEXT 7

EXODUS 6:9

וַיְדַבֵּר מֹשֶׁה כֵּן אֶל בְּנֵי יִשְׂרָאֵל, וְלֹא שָׁמְעוּ אֶל מֹשֶׁה מִקֹּצֶר רוּחַ וּמֵעֲבֹדָה קָשָׁה.

Moses spoke these words to the Children of Israel, but they did not hearken to Moses because of their suffering and their hard labor.

QUESTION FOR DISCUSSION

Have you ever had a conversation with someone and felt that the other *heard* you but didn't *listen* to you? How would you describe the difference?

TEXT 8

RABBI YEHOSHUA FALK KATZ,
SEFER ME'IRAT EINAYIM, CHOSHEN MISHPAT 17:15

וּסְבָרָא הוּא, כְּדֵי שֶׁיְּהֵא נוֹחַ דַּעַת בַּעֲלֵי דִין, וְלֹא יַעֲלֶה עַל לִבָּם שֶׁמָּא
הַדַּיָּינִים יִשְׂאוּ וְיִתְּנוּ בַּדִּין וְלֹא הֵבִינוּ טַעֲנָתָן . . .

וְעוֹד, שֶׁמָּא בֶּאֱמֶת הַדַּיָּינִים לֹא עָמְדוּ הֵיטֵב עַל דִּבְרֵי טַעֲנוֹתָן, וּבְשַׁנּוֹתָן
לִפְנֵי הַבַּעֲלֵי דִין יְעוֹרְרוּ אוֹתָן לוֹמַר כֹּה וְכֹה הָיוּ טַעֲנוֹתֵיהֶם.

The judges need to restate the arguments in order to put the litigants' minds at ease, so that they will not worry that the judges are deliberating the case without having properly understood their respective claims....

Moreover, it is entirely possible that the judges misunderstood the arguments. If this occurred, when the judges restate the arguments, the litigants will have the opportunity to correct the misunderstanding.

RABBI YEHOSHUA FALK HAKOHEN KATZ
1555–1614

Polish rabbi, Talmudist, and authority on Jewish law. Rabbi Falk is best known for his *Perishah* and *Derishah* commentaries on the *Arbaah Turim,* as well as *Sefer Me'irat Einayim* on the Code of Jewish Law. Rabbi Falk was a pupil of Rabbi Moshe Isserlis and served as head of the yeshiva in Lemberg, as well as on the Council of Four Lands, a central body of Jewish authority in Poland.

Exercise 4.6

You are about to engage in a conversation with another.

1   Take a moment before the conversation to remind yourself that listening is a skill that requires effort.

2   Refrain from thinking about what you want to say while the other is talking.

3   Invite the speaker, who has already completed the point, to elaborate on his or her experience or point of view.

4   Acknowledge and restate what the speaker said before offering your point of view.

TEXT 9

MIDRASH, *PESIKTA RABATI* 9

אָמַר הַקָּדוֹשׁ בָּרוּךְ הוּא: כְּשֶׁאֲנִי נוֹצֵחַ אֲנִי מַפְסִיד וּכְשֶׁאֲנִי נָצוּחַ אֲנִי מִשְׂתַּכֵּר.

נִצַּחְתִּי אֶת דּוֹר הַמַּבּוּל, לֹא אֲנִי הִפְסַדְתִּי שֶׁהֶחֱרַבְתִּי עוֹלָמִי? שֶׁנֶּאֱמַר "וַיִּמַח אֶת כָּל הַיְקוּם" (בְּרֵאשִׁית ז, כג). וְכֵן דּוֹר הַפְלָגָה וּסְדוֹמִיִּים.

אֲבָל בִּימֵי מֹשֶׁה שֶׁנּוּצַּחְתִּי, עָשִׂיתִי שָׂכַר, שֶׁלֹּא כִלִּיתִי אֶת יִשְׂרָאֵל.

הֱוֵי לַמְנַצֵּחַ - לְמִי שֶׁהוּא מְבַקֵּשׁ לְהִנָּצֵחַ.

G-d said, "When I am triumphant, I lose, and when I am triumphed over, I gain.

"I triumphed over the generation of the flood, but I lost, for I destroyed My world. As it states, 'And [the flood] blotted out all that there was' (Genesis 7:23). The same was true concerning the generation of the dispersion and the city of Sodom.

"However, in the days of Moses, I was triumphed over, but I gained in that I did not destroy Israel."

This is the meaning of the word, *Lamenatse'ach*, ["to the choirmaster"]. Let it be read as, "To Him Who desires to be triumphed over."

PESIKTA RABATI

A Midrash divided into a series of sections, as indicated by its title *Pesikta*, which means "section." It differs in structure from most other Midrashic texts, which are continuous commentaries to the Bible. It is called *Rabati* ("the greater"), probably in contrast to *Pesikta DeRav Kahana*. The opening of *Pesikta Rabati* indicates that it was compiled 777 years after the destruction of the Temple, circa 845.

TEXT 10A

THE REBBE, RABBI MENACHEM MENDEL SCHNEERSON, *IGROT KODESH* 20, P. 41

מֵאֲשֶׁר הִנְנִי קַבָּלַת מִכְתָּבָה . . . וְלַמְרוֹת סִגְנוֹן כְּתָבָהּ וְתוֹכְנוֹ, וְעוֹד יוֹתֵר לַמְרוֹת שֶׁהַמַּצָּב נִשְׁנָה כִּמְעַט בְּכָל מִכְתָּב מִמֶּנָּה, הֲרֵי לֹא אָבַדְתִּי חַס וְשָׁלוֹם תִּקְוָתִי, אֲשֶׁר סוֹף סוֹף לֹא רַק תִּרְאֶה אֶת הַטּוֹב בַּחַיִּים, כּוֹלֵל גַּם חַיֶּיהָ, אֶלָּא שֶׁבִּרְאִיָּה זוּ תָּבוֹא בְּהַרְגָּשָׁה בַּלֵּב.

וּבִפְרָט עַל פִּי סִגְנוֹן תּוֹרַת הַחֲסִידוּת, אֲשֶׁר בְּעוֹלָמֵנוּ זֶה הַכֹּל מְעוּרָב טוֹב
וָרַע, וְעַל הָאָדָם לִבְחוֹר מַה לְהַדְגִּישׁ וּבַמֶּה לְהִתְבּוֹנֵן, וּבַמֶּה לְהִתְעַנְיֵן, כִּי
בְּחַיֵּי כָּל אֶחָד וְאַחַת שְׁנֵי דְרָכִים יֶשְׁנָם, לִרְאוֹת אֶת הַטּוֹב הַסּוֹבֵב אוֹתוֹ
אוֹ וְכוּלִי . . .

וַהֲרֵי מְאַלְפֵנוּ סִיפּוּר חֲכָמֵינוּ זִכְרוֹנָם לִבְרָכָה, אֲשֶׁר אָדָם הָרִאשׁוֹן, עוֹד
קוֹדֶם הַגֵּירוּשׁ בִּהְיוֹתוֹ בְּגַן עֵדֶן, הִתְאוֹנֵן עַל עִנְיָנָיו, וּקְרָאוּהוּ כָּפוּי טוֹבָה,
וּבְנֵי וּבְנוֹת יִשְׂרָאֵל, שֶׁנִּמְצְאוּ בְּמַחֲנוֹת הַהֶסְגֵּר שֶׁל הָאַשְׁכְּנַזִים יְמַח
שְׁמָם וּבִתְקוּפָה הַכִּי אֲיוּמָה רַחֲמָנָא לִיצְלַן, בֵּרְכוּ בִּרְכַּת הַשַּׁחַר וְכוּלִי,
הוֹדָאָה וּבְרָכָה לְבוֹרֵא עוֹלָם וּמַנְהִיגוֹ, וַהֲרֵי סוֹף סוֹף כָּל אֶחָד וְאַחַת הוּא
בֵּין הַקְּצָווֹת הָאֲמוּרִים.

מוּבָן וְגַם פָּשׁוּט, שֶׁאֵין בְּהַנִּזְכַּר לְעֵיל חַס וְשָׁלוֹם עִנְיָן שֶׁל הַצַּדָּקַת הַדִּין עַל
מִי שֶׁהוּא, וּבִפְרָט וְכוּלִי, כִּי אִם הַדְגָּשַׁת הַמְּצִיאוּת כְּמוֹ שֶׁהִיא. וְהַנְּקוּדָה
- אֲשֶׁר אוֹפֶן וְסוּג חַיֵּי הָאָדָם, אִם חַיִּים מְלֵאִים שְׂבִיעַת רָצוֹן וְתוֹכֶן, אוֹ
בְּקַו הַהָפְכִי, תְּלוּיִ בְּמִדָּה חֲשׁוּבָה וּגְדוֹלָה - בִּרְצוֹן הָאָדָם, הַמּוֹשֵׁל בִּרְאִיַת
עֵין שִׂכְלוֹ לְהִסְתַּכֵּל לְצַד יָמִין אוֹ לְצַד שְׂמֹאל.

RABBI MENACHEM MENDEL SCHNEERSON
1902–1994

The towering Jewish leader of the 20th century, known as "the Lubavitcher Rebbe," or simply as "the Rebbe." Born in southern Ukraine, the Rebbe escaped Nazi-occupied Europe, arriving in the U.S. in June 1941. The Rebbe inspired and guided the revival of traditional Judaism after the European devastation, impacting virtually every Jewish community the world over. The Rebbe often emphasized that the performance of just one additional good deed could usher in the era of Mashiach. The Rebbe's scholarly talks and writings have been printed in more than 200 volumes.

I acknowledge receipt of your letter…. Despite the tone and content of your writing, and despite the fact that this repeats itself in almost all of your past letters, nevertheless, I have not lost hope that eventually you will appreciate the good in life, including the good in *your own* life, and that furthermore, this will impact your emotions and frame of mind.

In our world, everything consists of a mixture of good and bad, and human beings must choose which aspects they will emphasize and grant focus to. In everyone's life, there are two paths—to see the good, or to see the opposite….

How instructive is that which our sages tell us that Adam was an ingrate. Even before he was banished from the Garden of Eden, he complained about his circumstances. On the other hand, there were Jewish men and women who thanked and blessed the Creator and Orchestrator of the world and recited the morning blessings, while living through the most horrifying times in the German concentrations camps. Ultimately, everyone's circumstances will be somewhere *between* these two extremes.

Needless to say, my intention is not to imply that anyone deserves suffering, G-d forbid. My point is simply to underscore the reality, which can be summed up as follows: the type of lives that we live, whether full of satisfaction and meaning or the opposite, depends, in large measure, on our willpower, which dictates whether our "mental eyes" will focus on the positive or on the negative.

TEXT 10B

THE REBBE, RABBI MENACHEM MENDEL SCHNEERSON,
IBID., 12:270–271

בְּמַעֲנֶה עַל מִכְתָּבוֹ . . . בּוֹ כּוֹתֵב מַצָּבוֹ עַתָּה וְכֵן אֲשֶׁר כָּל מֶשֶׁךְ יְמֵי חַיָּיו לֹא רָאָה טוֹב, וּמְבַקֵּשׁ לְהַזְכִּירוֹ וְכֵן זוּגָתוֹ וִילִדֵיהֶם שֶׁיִּחְיוּ לִבְרָכָה.

וּכְנִרְאֶה שֶׁאֵינוֹ מַרְגִּישׁ בְּהַסְתִּירָה בְּמִכְתָּבוֹ עַצְמוֹ. כִּי אִישׁ אֲשֶׁר בּוֹרֵא עוֹלָם הִזְמִין לוֹ אֶת בַּת גִּילוֹ וּבֵרְכֶם בִּילָדִים - שְׁלִיטָ"א, יֹאמַר שֶׁלֹּא רָאָה טוֹב מִיָּמָיו, הֲרֵי הוּא כָּפוּי טוֹבָה בְּמִדָּה מַבְהִילָה . . . וַהֲרֵי מֵאוֹת וַאֲלָפִים מִבְּנֵי אָדָם מִתְפַּלְלִים בְּכָל יוֹם וְיוֹם לְהִתְבָּרֵךְ בִּפְרִי בֶטֶן, וְהָיוּ נוֹתְנִים אֶת כָּל אֲשֶׁר לָהֶם בִּשְׁבִיל בֵּן יָחִיד אוֹ בַּת יְחִידָה, וַעֲדַיִן לֹא זָכוּ לְזֶה - יְבָרְכֶם הַשֵּׁם יִתְבָּרֵךְ בְּמִלּוּי מִשְׁאֲלוֹת לְבָבָם לְטוֹבָה בְּקָרוֹב - וְהוּא אֲשֶׁר קִבֵּל בְּרָכָה זוֹ, וּכְנִרְאֶה מִבְּלִי תְּפִלָּה יְתֵירָה עַל הַדָּבָר, אֵינוֹ מַכִּיר בָּהָעוֹשֶׁר וְהָאוֹשֶׁר אֲשֶׁר בָּזֶה וְכוֹפֵל בְּמִכְתָּבוֹ כְּהָאָמוּר לְעֵיל! וְעוֹד מְסַיֵּים אֲשֶׁר אֵינוֹ מַאֲמִין חַס וְשָׁלוֹם שֶׁיַּעַזְרוּ לוֹ מִלְמַעְלָה, כִּי נִגְזַר חַס וְשָׁלוֹם שֶׁכָּל יָמָיו יִהְיוּ עֲנִיִּים וּמְרוּדִים!

מוּבָן שֶׁאֵין כַּוָּנָתִי לוֹמַר שֶׁהַפַּרְנָסָה צְרִיכָה לִהְיוֹת בְּצִמְצוּם אוֹ מַצָּב הַבְּרִיאוּת בַּחֲלִישׁוּת וְכוּ' . . . תִּקְוָתִי שֶׁשּׁוּרוֹתַי אֵלֶּה הַמְעַטּוֹת בְּכַמּוּת תַּסְפִּיקֶנָּה לְהָאִיר עֵינָיו לִרְאוֹת אֶת הַמַּצָּב כְּמוֹ שֶׁהוּא.

In response to your letter . . . in which you write about your current situation—that throughout your entire life you have not experienced good, and you request my blessing for yourself, your wife, and your children, may they all be well.

It seems that you do not sense the contradiction in your letter. For a man whom G-d has blessed with a wife and children to say that he has never seen any good is to be startlingly ungrateful.... Hundreds, even thousands of people pray every day to be blessed with children, and they would give everything they have to have a single son or daughter, but have not as of yet had their prayers answered—may G-d bless them that their hearts' wishes be fulfilled very soon. But you who received this blessing—and it seems that it came to you without any extra effort—apparently don't recognize the fortune and joy in the blessings you have. You write twice in your letter that you have never experienced any good, and you conclude your letter that you don't believe G-d will help you because it has been decreed (G-d forbid!) that you will be destitute all your life!

Understandably, my intention is not that one's livelihood ought to be meager or that one's health ought to be compromised, etc.... My hope is that these lines, brief in quantity, will suffice to enlighten you to see the situation as it really is.

QUESTIONS FOR DISCUSSION

- ► What seems to be similar about the two correspondents?

- ► How would you summarize the Rebbe's primary message in his responses?

TEXT 11

RABBI MENACHEM MENDEL OF LUBAVITCH, *IGROT KODESH*, P. 21

לְהַרְאוֹת בְּעַצְמוֹ תָּמִיד תְּנוּעוֹת מְשַׂמְחוֹת כְּאִלּוּ הוּא מָלֵא שִׂמְחָה בְּלִבּוֹ,
אַף עַל פִּי שֶׁאֵין בְּלִבּוֹ כֵּן בִּשְׁעַת מַעֲשֶׂה, וְסוֹפוֹ לִהְיוֹת כֵּן. וְהַטַעַם בָּזֶה הוּא
כִּי לְפִי הַמַּעֲשִׂים וְהַפְּעוּלוֹת אֲשֶׁר הָאָדָם עוֹשֶׂה, נִקְבַּע אַחַר כָּךְ בְּלִבָבוֹ.

At all times, assume a demeanor as if your heart were full of joy, even if, at the moment, this is far from the case. Such behavior will eventually lead you to truly feel happy, because behavior and action impact the heart.

Key Points

1 Successful relationships are crucial to our happiness, and they lie at the core of human identity. This is true for both extroverts and introverts.

2 Many Jewish observances are imbued with an ethos of genuine social connection. By embracing these, we open ourselves to more of the well-being that is derived from community and friendship.

3 Jewish sources are replete with teachings about working on our character. The underlying premise of these teachings is that we can choose to behave in specific ways even if our character predisposes us to act differently. Further, when we act a certain way multiple times, our disposition and character traits are eventually able to undergo change.

4 A number of traits hinder our ability to connect with others. Among them are

   a the tendency to be cynical about the motives of others;

   b the inability to tolerate those who have differing views; and

   c the unwillingness to genuinely listen to others.

5 If we want to build good relationships with others, we should get better at

   a attributing noble motives to people's behavior;

    b connecting with people who disagree with us by focusing on areas of agreement; and

    c listening when people speak to us and demonstrating our attentiveness by rephrasing what they have said.

6 Instead of regarding our opinions as absolute truths and fixed definitions of our personality, we can regard them as our current best attempt to arrive at the truth. This leaves us open to hearing a different perspective. With this mindset, disagreements can become productive links within a relationship.

7 Arrogance is the gateway to many character flaws. It is one of the causes of cynicism, being disagreeable, and the unwillingness to listen. By becoming less self-absorbed, there is more room for others and the happiness we can find by connecting with them.

8 When relationships lead to painful experiences, it is normal to be saddened, even as we understand that we will recover. At the same time, we must avoid falling into the trap of viewing all of life in a negative manner. We must remain tethered to reality, which includes focusing on the good in our lives. This balance allows for equilibrium and happiness despite the pain and difficulty.

9 Going through the motions of happiness can trigger emotions of happiness.

Appendix

TEXT 12

ED DIENER AND ROBERT BISWAS-DIENER, *HAPPINESS: UNLOCKING THE MYSTERIES OF PSYCHOLOGICAL WEALTH* (MALDEN, MASS.: BLACKWELL PUBLISHING, 2011), PP. 50–52

Relationships are themselves a crucial part of psychological wealth, without which you cannot be truly rich. Simply put, we need others to flourish. Indeed, the results of research on social relationships and happiness are clear on this point: healthy social contact is essential for happiness. Family relationships and close friendships are important to happiness.... In fact, the links between happiness and social contact are so strong that many psychologists think that humans are genetically wired to need one another....

In one study, for example, we collected mood data from people using the experience sampling method (ESM). Throughout the day, we signaled the research participants with random alarms, after which they would complete a short mood survey and indicate the type of situation they were in: Were they alone, or with other people?

ED DIENER, PHD
1946–

Psychologist and professor. Dr. Diener is a leading researcher in positive psychology who coined the expression "subjective well-being," or SWB, as the aspect of happiness that can be empirically measured. Noted for his research on happiness, he has earned the nickname "Dr. Happiness."

ROBERT BISWAS-DIENER, PHD
1972–

Positive psychologist. Biswas-Diener is the son of Edward Diener and is an instructor at Portland State University. Biswas-Diener's research focuses on income and happiness, culture and happiness, and positive psychology. Biswas-Diener's research has led him to many nations, including India, Greenland, Israel, Kenya, and Spain, and he has been called the "Indiana Jones of positive psychology." He sits on the editorial boards of the *Journal of Happiness Studies* and the *Journal of Positive Psychology.*

Initially, we suspected that introverts would be happier when they were alone and that extroverts would be happier when they were in a social setting. . . . Flying in the face of our prediction, both extroverts and introverts had more positive emotions when they were with other people. That's right: even introverts who have the reputation for being social wallflowers enjoyed themselves more when they were in social settings. Although it's true that extroverts spent a bit more time with other people, both groups showed more pleasant moods when they were engaged in social contact. Indeed, the introverts get as much boost from being with people as did extroverts. . . .

It's certainly not true that we would like to surround ourselves with other people all the time, but when we do, we tend to feel good.

TEXT 13

SONJA LYUBOMIRSKY, *THE MYTHS OF HAPPINESS*
(NEW YORK: PENGUIN BOOKS, 2014), P. 63

Most of the time, social support won't make a problem disappear, but it can go a long way in helping us address the problem, mitigate it, and lighten our emotional reaction to it.

In a clever study that supports this claim, researchers recruited volunteers who happened to be passing the base of a hill and were either alone or with a friend. Incredibly, those who were accompanied by a friend—especially a friend they were close to and knew a long time—judged the hill to be *less steep* than those who were alone.

Serving as a metaphor for the challenges of life . . . companions and confidants can make us feel that our problems and stresses are less steep as well.

SONJA LYUBOMIRSKY, PHD

Leading expert in positive psychology. Dr. Lyubomirsky is professor of psychology at the University of California, Riverside. Originally from Russia, she received her PhD in social/personality psychology from Stanford University. Her research on the possibility of permanently increasing happiness has been honored with various grants, including a million-dollar grant from the National Institute of Mental Health. She has authored *The How of Happiness* and, more recently, *The Myths of Happiness.*

TEXT 14

"LONELINESS IS A SERIOUS PUBLIC-HEALTH PROBLEM,"
THE ECONOMIST, SEPTEMBER 1, 2018

The Economist and the Kaiser Family Foundation (KFF), an American non-profit group focused on health, surveyed nationally representative samples of people in three rich countries. The study found that 9% of adults in Japan, 22% in America and 23% in Britain always or often feel lonely, or lack companionship, or else feel left out or isolated.

The findings complement academic research which uses standardised questionnaires to measure loneliness. One drawn up at the University of California, Los Angeles (UCLA), has 20 statements, such as "I have nobody to talk to," and "I find myself waiting for people to call or write." Responses are marked based on the extent to which people agree. Respondents with tallies above a threshold are classed as lonely. A study published in 2010 using this scale estimated that 35% of Americans over 45 were lonely.... In 2013 Britain's Office for National Statistics (ONS), by dint of asking a simple question, classed 25% of people aged 52 or over as "sometimes lonely" with an extra 9% "often lonely."

Further Study

Continue to explore the topics of happiness, positivity, and mental wellness:

The father is a respected rabbi who has counseled thousands. The son is a world-renowned psychologist who has plumbed the secrets of human behavior. Together, Rabbi Raphael Pelcovitz and Dr. David Pelcovitz have created a remarkable book that draws from the burgeoning field of Positive Psychology.

This book includes a brief collection of Torah sources on cognitive behavioral therapy; dialectical behavior therapy; general psychotherapy; anxiety, obsessions, compulsions, and depression; and mental health and well-being.

An inspiring and life-enriching tapestry woven from hundreds of stories, letters, anecdotes, and vignettes. *Positivity Bias* highlights how the Lubavitcher Rebbe, Rabbi Menachem M. Schneerson, of righteous memory, taught us to see ourselves, others, and the world around us.

Integrating spiritual, psychological, and religious truths, the founder of Gateway Rehabilitation Center, Dr. Twerski, draws upon his 40 years of experience as a psychiatrist, rabbi, and counselor to provide a year's worth of daily meditations filled with warmth, wisdom, and insight that will give the courage needed to live "one day at a time."

CONFLICT RESOLUTION

RABBI LORD JONATHAN SACKS

One of the hardest tasks of a leader—from prime ministers to parents—is conflict resolution. Yet it is also the most vital. Where there is leadership, there is long-term cohesiveness within the group, whatever the short-term problems. Where there is a lack of leadership—where leaders lack authority, grace, generosity of spirit and the ability to respect positions other than their own—then there is divisiveness, rancor, backbiting, resentment, internal politics and a lack of trust. Leaders are people who put the interests of the group above those of any subsection of the group. They care for, and inspire others to care for, the common good.

That is why an episode in this week's Parshah is of the highest consequence. It arose like this. The Israelites were on the last stage of their journey to the Promised Land. They were now situated on the east bank of the Jordan, within sight of their destination. Two of the tribes, Reuben and Gad, who had large herds and flocks of cattle, felt that the land they were currently on was ideal for their purposes. It was good grazing country. So they approached Moses and asked for permission to stay there rather than take up their share in the Land of Israel. They said: "If we have found favor in your eyes, let this land be given to your servants as our possession. Do not make us cross the Jordan."[1]

Moses was instantly alert to the danger. The two tribes were putting their own interests above those of the nation as a whole. They would be seen as abandoning the nation at the very time they were needed most. There was a war—in fact, a series of wars—to be fought if the Israelites were to inherit the Promised Land. As Moses put it to the tribes: "Should your fellow Israelites go to war while you sit here?

Why do you discourage the Israelites from crossing over into the land the L-rd has given them?"[2]

The proposal was potentially disastrous. Moses reminded the men of Reuben and Gad what had happened in the incident of the spies. The spies demoralized the people, ten of them saying that they could not conquer the land. The inhabitants were too strong. The cities were impregnable. The result of that one moment was to condemn an entire generation to die in the wilderness and to delay the eventual conquest by forty years. "And here you are, a brood of sinners, standing in the place of your fathers and making the L-rd even more angry with Israel. If you turn away from following Him, He will again leave all this people in the wilderness, and you will be the cause of their destruction."[3] Moses was blunt, honest and confrontational.

What then followed is a role model in negotiation and conflict resolution. The Reubenites and Gadites recognized the claims of the people as a whole and the justice of Moses' concerns. They propose a compromise. Let us make provisions for our cattle and our families, they say, and the men will then accompany the other tribes across the Jordan. They will fight alongside them. They will even go ahead of them. They will not return to their cattle and families until all the battles have been fought, the land has been conquered and the other tribes have received their inheritance. Essentially, they invoke what would later become a principle of Jewish law: *zeh neheneh ve-zeh lo chaser*, meaning that an act is permissible if "one side gains and the other side does not lose."[4] We will gain, say the two tribes, by having land good for our cattle, but the nation as a whole will not lose because we will be in the army, we will be in the front line, and we will stay there until the war has been won.

Moses recognizes the fact that they have met his objections. He restates their position to make sure he and they have understood the proposal and they are ready to stand by it. He extracts from them agreement to a *tenai kaful*, a double condition, both positive and negative: If we do this, these will be the consequences, but if we fail to do this, those will be

RABBI LORD JONATHAN SACKS, PHD (1948–2020)

Former chief rabbi of the United Kingdom. Rabbi Sacks attended Cambridge University and received his doctorate from King's College, London. A prolific and influential author, his books include *Will We Have Jewish Grandchildren?* and *The Dignity of Difference*. He received the Jerusalem Prize in 1995 for his contributions to enhancing Jewish life in the Diaspora, was knighted and made a life peer in 2005, and became Baron Sacks of Aldridge in 2009.

the consequences. He leaves them no escape from their commitment. The two tribes agree. Conflict has been averted. The Reubenites and Gadites achieve what they want, but the interests of the other tribes and of the nation as a whole have been secured. It was a model negotiation.

Quite how justified were Moses' concerns became apparent many years later. The Reubenites and Gadites did indeed fulfill their promise in the days of Joshua. The rest of the tribes conquered and settled Israel, while they (together with half the tribe of Manasseh) established their presence in Trans-Jordan. Despite this, within a brief space of time there was almost civil war.

Joshua 22 describes how, returning to their families and settling their land, the Reubenites and Gadites built "an altar to the L-rd" on the east side of the Jordan. Seeing this as an act of secession, the rest of the Israelites prepared to do battle against them. Joshua, in a striking act of diplomacy, sent Pinchas, the former zealot, now man of peace, to negotiate. He warned them of the terrible consequences of what they had done by, in effect, creating a religious center outside the Land of Israel. It would split the nation in two.

The Reubenites and Gadites made it clear that this was not their intention at all. To the contrary, they themselves were worried that in the future, the rest of the Israelites would see them living across the Jordan and conclude that they no longer wanted to be part of the nation. That is why they had built the altar, not to offer sacrifices, not as a rival to the nation's sanctuary, but merely as a symbol and a sign to future generations that they too were Israelites. Pinchas and the rest of the delegation were satisfied with this answer, and once again civil war was averted.

The negotiation between Moses and the two tribes in our Parshah follows closely the principles arrived at by the Harvard Negotiation Project, set out by Roger Fisher and William Ury in their classic text, *Getting to Yes*.[5] Essentially, they came to the conclusion that a successful negotiation must involve four processes:

1. *Separate the people from the problem.* There are all sorts of personal tensions in any negotiation. It is essential that these be cleared away first, so that the problem can be addressed objectively.
2. *Focus on interests, not positions.* It is easy for any conflict to turn into a zero-sum game: if I win, you lose. If you win, I lose. That is what happens when you focus on positions and the question becomes, "Who wins?" By focusing not on positions but on interests, the question becomes, "Is there a way of achieving what each of us wants?"
3. *Invent options for mutual gain.* This is the idea expressed halakhically as *zeh neheneh ve-zeh neheneh*, "both sides benefit." This comes about because the two sides usually have different objectives, neither of which excludes the other.
4. *Insist on objective criteria.* Make sure that both sides agree in advance to the use of objective, impartial criteria to judge whether what has been agreed has been achieved. Otherwise, despite all apparent agreement, the dispute will continue, both sides insisting that the other has not done what was promised.

Moses does all four. First he separates the people from the problem by making it clear to the Reubenites and Gadites that the issue has nothing to do with who they are, and everything to do with the Israelites' experience in the past, specifically the episode of the spies. Regardless of who the ten negative spies were and which tribes they came from, everyone suffered. No one gained. The problem is not about this tribe or that, but about the nation as a whole.

Second, he focused on interests, not positions. The two tribes had an interest in the fate of the nation as a whole. If they put their personal interests first, G-d would become angry and the entire people would be punished, the Reubenites and Gadites among them. It is striking how different this negotiation was from that of Korach and his followers. There, the whole argument was about positions, not interests—about who was entitled to be a leader. The result was collective tragedy.

Third, the Reubenites and Gadites then invented an option for mutual gain. If you allow us to make temporary provisions for our cattle and children, they said, we will not only fight in the army; we will be its advance guard. We will benefit, knowing that our request has been granted. The nation will benefit by our willingness to take on the most demanding military task.

Fourth, there was an agreement on objective criteria. The Reubenites and Gadites would not return to the east bank of the Jordan until all the other tribes were safely settled in their territories. And so it happened, as narrated in the book of Joshua:

Then Joshua summoned the Reubenites, the Gadites and the half-tribe of Manasseh, and said to them, "You have done all that Moses the servant of the L-rd commanded, and you have obeyed me in everything I commanded. For a long time now—to this very day—you have not deserted your fellow Israelites, but have carried out the mission the L-rd your G-d gave you. Now that the L-rd your G-d has given them rest as He promised, return to your homes in the land that Moses the servant of the L-rd gave you on the other side of the Jordan."[6]

This was, in short, a model negotiation, a sign of hope after the many destructive conflicts in the book of Bamidbar, as well as a standing alternative to the many later conflicts in Jewish history that had such appalling outcomes.

Note that Moses succeeds, not because he is weak, not because he is willing to compromise on the integrity of the nation as a whole, not because he uses honeyed words and diplomatic evasions, but because he is honest, principled, and focused on the common good. We all face conflicts in our lives. This is how to resolve them.

Rabbisacks.org
Reprinted with permission of the author

Endnotes

1. Numbers 32:5.

2. Numbers 32:6–7.

3. Numbers 32:14–15.

4. Talmud, Bava Kamma 20b.

5. Roger Fisher and William Ury, *Getting to Yes: Negotiating Agreement Without Giving In* (Random House Business, 2011).

6. Joshua 22:1–4.

JewishU is an academy that provides students with the most effective platform to gain a comprehensive Jewish education alongside their standard college education.

JewishU offers dozens of unique classes that demystify everything Jewish. From history to philosophy and everything in between, there is no better place to begin or enhance your Jewish education in a relaxed and welcoming environment.

All courses are presented locally, easily fit into your schedule and offer valuable JewishU credits with flexible redemption opportunities, plus the opportunity to earn a JewishU certificate in Jewish Studies.

This Jewish education is 100% subsidized, and rewarding.

Simply enroll once; then whenever your schedule allows, select your topic of choice, learn, earn, and repeat. You can easily manage your courses, progress, and credits online.

Perhaps the best part is that each course consists of just four classes, with zero homework. We know you want to learn more about yourself, your history and heritage, but we also know you're busy. Like really busy. That's why we created JewishU.

JewishU

JewishU Locations

As of this printing, JewishU has chapters at 35 campus Chabad centers. JewishU grows every year and may now include additional locations.

NORTHEAST

Binghamton University
Rabbi Zalman & Rochel Chein
607-797-0015
chabadofbinghamton.com

Boston University
Rabbi Shmuel & Chana Posner
617-424-1190
chabadboston.org

City College of New York
Rabbi Yudi & Chanie Shmotkin
917-531-8722
jewishccny.com

Cornell University
Rabbi Dovid & Miri Birk
607-319-0874
chabadcornell.com

Hamilton College
Rabbi Didy & Devorah Waks
315-925-7613
chabadclinton.com

Penn State Undergrads
Rabbi Hershy & Miri Gourarie
814-441-9985
thepsjews.com

Towson University
Rabbi Mendy & Sheiny Rivkin
410-825-0779
jewishtowson.com

University of Pennsylvania
Rabbi Levi & Nechama Haskelevich
215-746-6115
lubavitchhouse.com

University of Rochester
Rabbi Asher & Devorah Leah Yaras
585-503-9224
campuschabad.com

Wesleyan University
Rabbi Levi & Chana Schectman
860-704-9595
chabadwesleyan.org

SOUTHEAST

Florida Gulf Coast University - Undergrads
Rabbi Mendel & Shternie Gordon
347-452-0489
chabadfgcu.com

Florida State University
Rabbi Schneur Zalman & Chana Oirechman
850-523-9294
chabadtallahassee.com

University of Central Florida
Rabbi Chaim Boruch & Rivkie Lipskier
407-949-8838
jewishucf.com

University of Miami
Rabbi Mendy & Henchi Fellig
305-206-4013
jewishcanes.com

MIDWEST

Carnegie Mellon University
Rabbi Shlomo & Chani Silverman
412-772-8505
chabadofcmu.com

Michigan State University
Rabbi Benzion & Simi Shemtov
347-515-4079
jewishspartans.com

Northwestern University
Rabbi Mendy & Ariella Weg
847-869-8060
nuchabad.org

University of Chicago
Rabbi Yossi & Baila Brackman
773-955-8672
chabaduchicago.com

University of Illinois at Chicago
Rabbi Bentzion & Chani Shemtov
312-733-1383
chabaduic.com

University of Kansas
Rabbi Zalman &
Mrs. Nechama Dina Tiechtel
785-832-8672
jewishku.com

University of Pittsburgh
Rabbi Shmuel & Chasi Rothstein
443-525-4212
10172.centers.chabad.org

University of Wisconsin-Madison
Rabbi Mendel & Henya Matusof
608-257-1757
uwchabad.com

SOUTH

American University
Rabbi Yehoshua & Esti Hecht
202-465-4601
chabadau.com

George Mason University
Rabbi Mendel & Raizel Deitsch
571-279-2587
chabadgmu.com

Kennesaw State University
Rabbi Zalman & Nechami Charytan
770-400-9255
chabadkennesaw.org

WEST COAST

California Polytechnic State University
Rabbi Chaim Leib & Miki Hilel
805-229-1836
chabadslo.com

Chapman University
Rabbi Eliezer & Mushky Gurary
657-333-0989
jewishchapman.com

Claremont Colleges
Rabbi Yossi & Rochel Matusof
909-257-9941
claremontchabad.com

University of California at Santa Cruz
Rabbi Shlomo & Devorah Leah Chein
831-471-9123
jewcsc.com

University of Oregon
Rabbi Berel & Rivkah Gurevitch
541-801-8653
jewisheugene.org

INTERNATIONAL

Queen's University
Rabbi Yisroel & Esther Simon
613-770-1884
chabadstudentcentre.ca

University of Birmingham
Rabbi Yossi & Rivki Cheruff
7805 092236
birminghamuchabad.com

University of British Columbia
Rabbi Chalom & Esti Loeub
778-712-7703
chabadubc.com

University of Guelph
Rabbi Raphi & Mussie Steiner
519-760-2857
jewishguelph.org

CHABAD ON CAMPUS INTERNATIONAL

FINANCE COMMITTEE

Adam Semler, Chair
Former CFO & COO,
York Capital Management

Howard Morgan
CEO, First Round Capital

Renato Negrin
Portfolio Manager, Millennium Partners

STEERING COMMITTEE

Rabbi Shlomo Silverman, Chair
Administration, Chair
Chabad at Carnegie Mellon University

Rabbi Berl Goldman
Shlichus Advancement, Chair
Chabad at University of Florida

Rabbi Chaim Leib Hilel
Student Engagement, Educational Instruction
Chabad at California Polytechnic
State University

Rabbi Shua Rosenstein
Chabad at Yale University

Rabbi Menachem Schmidt
Chabad on Campus Vaad, President
Chabad at the University of Pennsylvania

Rabbi Eli Simon
Shluchim and Shluchos Support, Chair
Chabad at Manchester Universities

Rabbi Shmuli Slonim
Chabad at Rice University

Rabbi Zalman Tiechtel
Student Engagement, Educational
Experience, Chair
Chabad at University of Kansas

—

Chava Backman
Student Engagement,
Educational Experiences
Chabad at University of South Florida

Rivki Cheruff
Shlichus Advancement, Chair
Chabad at University of Birmingham

Miri Gourarie
Administration, Chair
Chabad Undergrads at Penn State University

Miriam Lipskier
Chabad at Emory University

Sarah Rivkin
Shluchim and Shluchos Support, Chair
Chabad at Tulane University

Simi Shemtov
Chabad at Michigan State University

TEAM

Rabbi Yossy Gordon
Chief Executive Officer

Avi Weinstein
Chief Operating Officer

Thom Waye
Chief Strategy Officer

FINANCE

Rabbi Moshe C. Dubrowski
Vice President of Finance

Rivka Batashvili
CPA, Accounting Manager

Raizel Barber
Bookkeeping Associate

DEVELOPMENT

Moshe Angyalfi
Vice President of Development

Rabbi Mendy Cheruff
Director of Donor Relations

Basya Soffer
Development Manager

Shoshana Ross MA
Director of Data Analytics & Reporting

ADMINISTRATION

Rabbi Levi Rabin
Vice President of Administration

Vanessa Goldberg
Director of Marketing

Fraidy Barber
Manager of Strategic Grants

Mushky Rosenblum
Marketing Manager

Leah Zucker
Office and Customer Service Manager

STUDENT ENGAGEMENT

Rabbi Shlomie Chein
Vice President of Student Engagement

Rabbi Dubi Rabinowitz
Director of Sinai Scholars Society

Rabbi Yossi Witkes
Director of Virtual Experiences

Rabbi Ephraim Merovitch
Director of Resources and Partnerships

Rochel Munitz
Administrative Assistant to
Student Engagement

Mussi Rabinowitz
Sinai Scholars Coordinator

Manya Sperlin
Sinai Scholars Content Coordinator

Chana Zedek
Internal Processes Manager

Devorah Zlatopolsky
Sinai Scholars Society Coordinator

SHLICHUS SUPPORT & ADVANCEMENT

Avi Weinstein
VP of Shlichus Support and Advancement

Nechoma Dina Dubrowski
Director of Shluchim & Shluchos Support

Rabbi Moshe C. Dubrowski
Director of Shluchim Support

Miriam Minsky
Director of Shlichus
Advancement Operations

DEPARTMENT COMMITTEES

SHLUCHIM & SHLUCHOS SUPPORT

Rabbi Eli Simon, Chair
Chabad at Manchester Universities

Rabbi Eliezer Gurary
Chabad at Chapman University

Rabbi Meir Simcha Rubashkin
Chabad at SUNY College at Oneonta

Rabbi Shaul Wertheimer
Chabad at Queens College

—

Sarah Rivkin, Chair
Chabad at Tulane University

Matti Banon
Chabad at Université de Montreal

Mussy Posner
Chabad at Northeastern University

Runya Wagner
Chabad at University of Southern California

SHLICHUS ADVANCEMENT

Rabbi Berl Goldman, Chair
Chabad at University of Florida

Rabbi Chaim Boyarsky
Chabad at University of Ottawa

Rabbi Yochanan Rivkin
Chabad at Tulane University

Rabbi Dovid Tiechtel
Chabad at University of Illinois
at Urbana-Champaign

—

Rivki Cheruff, Chair
Chabad at University of Birmingham

Rosie Lipskier
Chabad at University of Alabama

STUDENT ENGAGEMENT EDUCATIONAL EXPERIENCES

Rabbi Zalman Tiechtel, Chair
Chabad at University of Kansas

Rabbi Zalman Bluming
Chabad at Duke University &
Links Educational Director

Rabbi Hershy Gourarie
Chabad Undergrads at Penn State University

Rabbi Eli Moshe Levitansky
Chabad at S. Monica College

Rabbi Hersh Loschak
Chabad at Rowan University

Rabbi Mendel Matusof
Chabad at University of Wisconsin-Madison

—

Chava Backman
Chabad at University of South Florida

Shifra Sharfstein
Chabad at Georgia Institute of Technology

Simi Shemtov
Chabad at Michigan State University

STUDENT ENGAGEMENT EDUCATIONAL INSTRUCTION

Rabbi Levi Friedman
Chabad at Florida International University

Rabbi Moshe Leib Gray
Chabad at Dartmouth College

Rabbi Chaim Leib Hilel
Chabad at California Polytechnic
State University

Rabbi Zev Johnson
Chabad at University of Texas at Austin

Rabbi Yossi Lazaroff
Chabad at Texas A&M University

Rabbi Levi Raichik
Chabad at Ohio University

Rabbi Shmuli Rothstein
Chabad at University of Pittsburgh

Rabbi Shmuel Teichtel
Chabad at Arizona State University

Rabbi Shmuly Weiss
Chabad at McGill University

—

Yocheved Boyarsky
Chabad at University of Ottawa

Chani Shemtov
Chabad at University of Illinois at Chicago

Zelly Refson
Savannah College of Art & Design

ADMINISTRATION

Rabbi Shlomo Silverman, Chair
Chabad at Carnegie Mellon University

Rabbi Zalman Charytan
Chabad at Kennesaw State University

Rabbi Didy Waks
Chabad at Hamilton College

Rabbi Yaakov Zar
Chabad House Bowery

—

Miri Gourarie, Chair
Chabad Undergrads at Penn State University

Shlomit Epstein
Chabad at University of South Carolina

Rivka Raichik
Chabad at Brooklyn College

Chanie Zwiebel
Chabad at Virginia Polytechnic Institute

THE ROHR JEWISH LEARNING INSTITUTE

AN AFFILIATE OF MERKOS L'INYONEI CHINUCH,
THE EDUCATIONAL ARM OF THE CHABAD-LUBAVITCH MOVEMENT
832 EASTERN PARKWAY, BROOKLYN, NY 11213

The Jewish Learning Multiplex

Brought to you by the Rohr Jewish Learning Institute

In fulfillment of the mandate of the Lubavitcher Rebbe, of blessed memory, whose leadership guides every step of our work, the mission of the Rohr Jewish Learning Institute is to transform Jewish life and the greater community through the study of Torah, connecting each Jew to our shared heritage of Jewish learning.

While our flagship program remains the cornerstone of our organization, JLI is proud to feature additional divisions catering to specific populations, in order to meet a wide array of educational needs.

The Rohr JEWISH LEARNING INSTITUTE

a subsidiary of **Merkos L'Inyonei Chinuch,**
the adult educational arm of the Chabad-Lubavitch movement

An academy by Chabad on Campus International, making Jewish education accessible, structured, and rewarding for Jewish college students.

An exclusive fellowship, in partnership with Chabad on Campus International, enabling students to explore the fundamentals of Judaism.

Torah Studies provides a rich and nuanced encounter with the weekly Torah reading.

Jewish teens forge their identity as they engage in Torah study, social interaction, and serious fun.

The Rosh Chodesh Society gathers Jewish women together once a month for intensive textual study.

TorahCafe.com provides an exclusive selection of top-rated Jewish educational videos.

This yearly event rejuvenates mind, body, and spirit with a powerful synthesis of Jewish learning and community.

Participants delve into our nation's past while exploring the Holy Land's relevance and meaning today.

Select affiliates are invited to partner with peers and noted professionals, as leaders of innovation and excellence.

Machon Shmuel is an institute providing Torah research in the service of educators worldwide.

Made in the USA
Coppell, TX
01 October 2021

63316677R00074